Mai Serhan is a Palestinian writer who grew up in Egypt. She is the author of *CAIRO: the undelivered letters*, winner of the 2022 Center for Book Arts Poetry Award, and *I Have Never Been to the Place Where I'm From, But I Will Imagine it For Us*, a finalist for the 2022 Narratively Memoir Prize. She holds an MSt in creative writing from the University of Oxford, and has studied at NYU and AUC. She lives in Cairo.

I Can Imagine It for Us
A Palestinian Daughter's Memoir

Mai Serhan

The American University in Cairo Press
Cairo   New York

First published in 2025 by
The American University in Cairo Press
113 Sharia Kasr el Aini, Cairo, Egypt
420 Lexington Avenue, Suite 1644, New York, NY 10170
www.aucpress.com

Copyright © 2025 by Mai Serhan

All rights reserved. No part of this publication may be
reproduced, stored in a retrieval system, or transmitted in any
form or by any means, electronic, mechanical, photocopying,
recording, or otherwise, without the prior written permission of
the publisher.

ISBN 978 1 649 03459 5

Library of Congress Cataloging-in-Publication Data

Names: Serhan, Mai, author.
Title: I can imagine it for us : a Palestinian daughter's memoir /
    Mai Serhan.
Identifiers: LCCN 2025031308 | ISBN 9781649034601
    (hardback) | ISBN 9781649034595 (paperback) | ISBN
    9781649034618 (epub) | ISBN 9781649034625 (adobe pdf)
Subjects: LCSH: Serhan, Mai. | Women, Palestinian Arab--Egypt--
    Biography. | LCGFT: Autobiographies.
Classification: LCC DT72.P35 S47 2026

1 2 3 4 5   29 28 27 26 25

Designed by David G. Hanna

For Baba

Part 1

Beirut, 2001

I am twenty-four years old when they amputate Baba's foot. He will drag it halfway around the world for one more year, but for now he has no choice but to stop and convalesce, with me by his side.

The family apartment in Beirut has three bedrooms, ours flanked by two others. The one where my uncle, Amo Jamal, sleeps is on the left. He's knocked out at noon, too much to drink the night before, the decades before. His liver will keep him supine, doused until it's done with its daunting task of detoxification. The one on the far right is where my grandmother, Teta Ibtihaj, lies staring at the ceiling. Her pasts are all catching up with her now, though she no longer wishes to remember. Lying in this haze thick as the smoke from that day when the tobacco fields turned to ash, she's regressing to that time and place, wondering where she is and who I am when I check in on her. Thankfully her Alzheimer's will protect her from one more year of great loss.

The middle bedroom where Baba and I lie on two single beds is austere, or maybe it's his austerity that is stripping the walls bare. There's a cupboard, but the room is dim all around, and I no longer recall a window.

Two plates of za'tar manakeesh and sliced cucumbers arrive lacking their usual luster, or maybe it's just me feeling blue. I eat while he reads the morning papers, then I bury my head in the papers, too. The South Lebanon Army has just collapsed and Hezbollah are advancing fast while Israel is withdrawing its troops from Lebanon six weeks before its July deadline. Lebanon's faltering banking system. An op-ed about a country slipping and state failure. None of this is what catches my eye, though.

A year earlier my father was standing on a foot that was no longer breathing, and no one knew. I had just completed a degree in English & Comparative Literature and graduated top of my class. I told him I wanted to pursue my graduate studies.

In what?

In literature.

Again?

No, a master's degree.

He looked at me like he would a child pestering him about a toy in a toy shop.

I am not paying tuition for you to read more stories. What catches my eye now is an ad, a call for a scholarship and a chance to win a full ride at SOAS University of London. I broach the subject again, and he turns to face me. He's unabashed by his debilitation, and his jaundiced eyes rimmed in red chill me.

You are not going anywhere.

But Baba, listen. I am a straight-A student. I'll do—

No, you listen: You have three options. Either you go back to Cairo to live with your mother, come back with me to China, or stay here in Lebanon with Teta.

He reaches for his pack of Rothmans. I grab the lighter.

Please listen—my uncles, they've sent my cousins
     abroad to study. Maya is in drama school in
     New York City. And Zena[1], she—
He tries to grab the lighter from my hand, but I get up,
take a step back. He tries to get up too, but he can't. His
body looks more and more like the fossil of a dinosaur.
His leg, now bandaged and propped on pillows, is missing five toes and the ball of the foot. He wants to walk
and keep walking. He's not built to stay in one place.
Instead, he says,

    And you want to be a whore like your cousins?

Shenzhen, 2000

Men from Bilad al-Sham use the word *mara* when referring to a woman. It is not a derogatory word in their culture, but in Egyptian, *mara* means *whore*.

It's the year before the amputation, and I tag along behind Baba and his Palestinian client up the busy streets of Shenzhen feeling very much like a *mara*, though I'm halfway around the world, though I am nowhere near Egypt nor the Levant. Ever since the men met, they have closed ranks and left me out. Perhaps it's because of my hair, my body. Perhaps it's because of my breasts. Whatever it is, I am made to feel like dangerous cargo amongst these men, a discomfort.

It's my second day in China and everything is novel, everything is a sensory overload, like I've tapped into an augmented reality. On my right, counterfeit designer merchandise is lined up along the sidewalk before storefronts decked with avant-garde streetwear: hip-hop inspired Chinese silhouettes, corsets embroidered with dragons and fish, anime and manga prints on vintage t-shirts. On my left, docks teem with freight ships and black smoke, heaving the moist odor of deep-fried chicken feet.

Baba and his client enter a café and sit next to each other. I watch them order coffees and fill an ashtray with cigarette butts. I listen to them make deals, lock orders, discuss containers, shipments, commissions. I'm fresh off the boat. Only two days ago, I was in Cairo. I want to interrupt, to tell him it's hot and humid and I hadn't packed for this weather, that I need flip-flops instead of these socks and sneakers, but Baba wants me to listen, sit quietly, invisibly. They finish their meeting and a pack of Rothmans between them and carry their conversation back to the street. I spot a large container of vintage t-shirts. A cardboard sign reads, "3 for $1."

Baba, can I have a dollar? I ask.

He stops, inconvenienced, and starts to haggle with the old woman. He wants all three t-shirts for fifty cents. She waves her hand, a firm no. He chucks the t-shirts back in the container and walks off. I stand in place, waiting to see if he'll turn back, acknowledge me. He doesn't.

I follow him until we reach his Shenzhen address, an office apartment on the thirty-third floor of a skyscraper. At the entrance, the security guard gawks. We're a rare sight, I get it—especially me. It's the year 2000 and Chairman Mao might be long gone, but it's still the early days of China's global emergence. There are no tourists in sight. Middle Eastern traders like my father might've started to trickle in in search of business opportunities, but me? I have no business being here.

I pick up the pace, ask Baba to slow down. I want to go back, I have some needs, I tell him, and he should stop and attend to me. He tells me, you are here to learn the ropes of the business, but instead all you want to do is shop. He's shouting, and I hate this scene playing out in front of the security guard. I want him to stop. I use the Egyptian word for shouting: *ga'ar*. My father mistakes it for the verb *to bray*, like a donkey.

You're calling your father a donkey, you little shit, he says and, before I know it, slaps me right across the face. The elevator shoots up like mercury in a thermometer, and I am feverish. I am prepared to set everything on fire, and apparently, so is he.

You can't. You can't do this. You can't hit me.
You've fucked us up, fucked us all up.
Me coming to China was your last chance to make it right.
I'm going back to Egypt.
I want my mum.

> Yeah, you go. You're her children.
> I look at you and see nothing of me.
> Don't even understand your language.
> Your mother's language.

Stop.

> Fucking Egyptian.

He rages at a distant point beyond him and me, at the burnt fields, at the bombs once dropping down from the sky into Ayn al-'Asal spring. He rages at the dynamite under Teta's kitchen once ripping the vine leaves and women's banter into a million shreds, at the fact that he will always be a renegade. Even amongst his family, a renegade.

Thirty-three floors up seem like ground floor to eternity, and I can never un-hear what he's just said. His words are dark, unnatural, shambolic, and this tight elevator we find ourselves trapped in is all these words, burning.

On the thirty-third floor, the elevator doors finally open. Baba unlocks his office apartment. I storm in, into his scant kitchen stacked with canned fava beans and hummus, his bedroom for two, his office. I am howling, my voice is a deep earth rumble, and I begin to destroy. I smash everything in sight, his fax machine, his computers, throw all the files on the shelves on the floor. I unhinge his desk drawers and rip away at business cards, invoices, contracts, bank transfer slips.

Then I call +2 02, I call Egypt, my mum. I want to tell her what he's done, what he's always done, that he's done it again.

Sweetheart, I am sorry. Please.

He holds my small shoulders in his big hands to steady me, but everywhere is shudder, clatter. I redial and redial, but this mist over Shenzhen is boundless and the line won't connect. *Please. I am sorry. Please.* This mist, it won't let me dial home. I am far, stuck, cut off. I am homesick, whatever home means.

Acre, pre-1948

I have never been to the place where I am from, but I can imagine it for us, Baba, for you and me. Memory might fail us more than seventy years on, but I have read all the stories you denied me, tinkered with all the words, stored endless images I can now mix and match to piece it all together. I know what antiheroes are made of and that their journeys are on a perpetual loop. I know that in a story, space can be the one character you can never forget.

Your home—you were four years old when they chased you out through thousands of orchards. May 21, 1948, was the last time you saw Umm Ahmad, your nanny. Before that, you were used to her carrying you everywhere she went, coiled close to her chest like you were in a womb, and the village folks mistook you for a girl. Yes, you had a nanny and long hair. You had cooks who pickled your olives and cleaners who cleaned a ten-bedroom family home, washerwomen who soaked your soiled clothes in hot water and bay leaves, and farmers who sowed your land and milled your grains. The whole village was at your service, once.

Do you remember that man who arrived in al-Kabri with a map? He opened it before a farmer and asked him to show him your father's land, Faris Serhan's. The farmer folded the map and gave it back to the man, it was of no use, and said, all you see, as far as the eye can see, belongs to Faris Serhan.

Don't believe it when they tell you the Garden of Eden is a celestial place. It is not. Those four rivers running under Man's feet, they were all right here in your village, once. A spring in Arabic is called *ayn*, as in eye. Look back and you will see. The eyes of al-Kabri: Ayn al-'Asal, Ayn al-Mafshuh, Ayn al-Fawwar, Ayn Kabri. Together they watered the whole of Acre and formed the largest water source in Palestine. Ayn al-'Asal was five meters wide by your father's mill. It was ice-cold in the summer and steaming hot in winter, like bubbling honeycomb. At night, Umm Ahmad sang to you while the waters flowed through the meandering fields and formed a sweet, lulling sound around the village. In the morning, she dipped your feet in and you splashed your happy legs the way geese splashed in the glistening sun, droplets forming diamonds on their feathers.

There were lots of mills along those springs: The al-Rayyis mill by al-'Asal, one by Ga'aton near the ancient ruins, al-Shufinneyeh, al-'Assafiyyeh, al-Drabseh, Umm al-Far, al-Minwat by Abu Laziq canal north of the village, and al-Serhan. In the meadows of Galilee, north of al-Kabri, was a water tank. It was twenty meters deep, ten meters wide, and held all the winter rain that watered the tobacco fields on the hills. It was where the cattle went to quench their thirst.

There was enough water for all there, Baba, for the wild carobs Teta turned to syrup for her winter home desserts, for the bitter orange infused in your cold drink, for the catnip along the banks that she plucked from its white flower to mix in a cool summer salad. All kinds

11

of fruit, too. Seven kinds of figs, the all-summer sweet, the one with black skin and red flesh, the sour one with light skin, the one with green skin and a rectangular seed. The women in your kitchen mixed the figs with walnuts, almonds, and sugar then boiled it all and stored it in clay pots for breakfast. Three kinds of olives, too, covered the eastern and northwestern hills: the big black ones with a small pit, marinated in Acre sea salt and lemon or pressed for extra virgin olive oil, the ones with big pits, and the green ones with small pits. All those olives soaked in winter rain right on time for the harvest in October. The farmers beat the branches with long sticks and shook them until the olives dropped. They dropped on large bamboo mats rolled out for them. The farmers loaded them into sacks and headed to the olive oil press, your press east of al-Kabri. When they were done, they made rosaries out of their pits to sell in Jerusalem and used the tree branches to make beams for homes and village walls.

It might seem to you that life is an inferno you cannot escape, but there once were four seasons. Look back, wherever your eyes fall, your heart drops too: In winter, rain poured like a waterfall, bringing the mudbrick. Your brothers, with bouncy locks and brilliant teeth, stripped down and jumped in the spring. Their bodies made of mud, washed in mud, drifted with the water and soaked in the rain. They soaked with the jojoba and oak trees that left a trail of perfume in the breeze. In spring, a multi-colored terrain of citrus yellow and henna red, and a green flying carpet to the east and northwest. You were on the rooftop under a fountain of stars on your father's lap watching the older kids jump from neighbors' roof to roof. Summer, nature's wedding and harvest time for lentils, sesame, and corn. At sunset, lights the color of peach orchards, and the road was lit with candles made of honey wax. At dawn, the farmers loaded the trucks with the land's bellyful of flowers and headed out to sell to the neighboring towns. Fall, a northern wind brought dust and dry leaves. The villagers raised their hands in prayer, asking God to calm the gust for the sake of the bobwhite, the starling, and the fowl. The fowl each laid ten eggs a go, enough to feed your entire household every morning.

Your house, Baba, Acre's command post of old Jerusalem stone, with delicate arches and tall pillars, was surrounded by cinchona trees. Their flowers, red, rose above the courtyard and the divan where the village elders met, over the ten balconies and the stairway windows.

There were enough views for all ten bedrooms. The ones for you and your siblings and the ones for all your uncles and aunts and all your cousins: Ahmed Serhan, Amina Serhan, Zakiyyeh Serhan, Amto Fatimeh, Amto Khayriyyeh, Amto Umm Yassir, Amto Umm Bassem, your grandmother, Sitti Umm Faris, and the tenth room, reserved for the village chief and his wife, Faris Serhan and Ibtihaj al-Qadi.

Cairo, 1969

People marry for different reasons. Some meet and fall in love, some tick all the right boxes for each other—religion, education, wealth, family name—and some are arranged. My parents married in 1969, for no good reason.

My mother's nickname is Nana. She was a pretty girl from Cairo, only twenty, her body wafer-thin. Daddy's girl, she never lived anywhere but home. Her mother, with rollers in her hair, would sew her dresses and, on an ironing board with floral prints, would press their frills warm. Nizar, my father, was a university dropout. No job, no land, but a big family name, once, and an after-life in Beirut.

Beirut in the 1960s—glamorous, infamous. Five-star hotels by the Mediterranean, nightclubs on Rue de Phénicie, and casinos in the Jounieh mountains with Brigitte Bardot and Omar Sharif at the corner table. Nana, still green, saw the world through rose-tinted shades. Wowed by the unknown, she must have thought, Beirut, so fancy, and so what if this suitor was without a land? She made homelessness an exotic place, and of his Levantine ways, a novelty. Something cool to tell her friends who had a home, like her. As for Nizar, he should've known after losing home that forever is never a way of life. Yet he saw Nana and dialed +961. He called his mother, Ibtihaj, in Beirut, to say I have met the one, and so what if she's Egyptian, so what if she'd never lived anywhere but home? I won't come back unless you let me marry her. Ibtihaj al-Qadi could not take another loss, so she hopped on a plane bound for Cairo with two wedding bands and a diamond ring to keep her son.

Nizar went back to school, for Nana. He studied television directing in Cairo, not because he had any interest in it, but because he had no interest in anything else. Nana was all he was interested in, and a degree, any degree, was how he was going to build his dream home with her.

Finally, he graduated. They celebrated their wedding at the Shepheard Hotel, and his family flew in from Beirut to meet Nana. In a black-and-white photo now in my possession, they all stand pretty in 1960s hairdos and eye makeup like Twiggy. She seems to fit right in among her new Palestinian sisters-in-law, a perfect addition to the lineup of beautiful women the Serhan sons had married. In that same photo, famous belly dancer Soheir Zaki shimmies before a smiling bride and groom.

They did not smile for long. Their honeymoon in Beirut is where his hands betrayed all his hidden strife. But Nana, she was daddy's girl, she was wafer-thin, homesick, morning sick. She was nauseous before she threw up once, two times, before the gynecologist confirmed, she was pregnant.

They moved to the Gulf, to Abu Dhabi, where Nizar worked as a television director and Nana, knowing by now that forever is never a way of life, had one child, then two. They had Nermin and me.

Abu Dhabi, 1981

Abu Dhabi is desert roads, expat compounds, and sports cars in 1981. That's where we all live when we are still we. Everything else is just one in a vast and untouched desert: One international school, one supermarket, one hospital. But there are a lot of us in that compound too, flanked by Palestinian uncles, aunts, and cousins left and right. Doors open day and night and Arabic coffee making the rounds for family and extended family. They take over the dining room, the kitchen, and the living room. They cook, gossip, fight, belly dance, talk politics, television always on in the background with a war blazing.

It's late when the doors finally close on the four of us. Nermin is ten and I am four. We both wear Scratch n Smell t-shirts in strawberry and raspberry scents. She kneels upright, the light of the TV a silver flicker on her face. Baba has me on his lap, and he whispers in my ear:

Tell her, Hey, TV head.

Hey, TV head, I repeat after him.

I want to tell you something.

He wants to tell you something.

Nermin is used to it. She tries her hardest to ignore it. He goes on:

Tell her I am not her real father. Tell her I found her under a tree.

> Baba is not your real father, I repeat, he found you under a tree.
>
> Please stop, she says.
>
> Tell her, your real name is not Nermin, it's Fawziyya.
>
> I laugh, Fawziyya, Fawziyya, Baba is not your real dad.
>
> Tell her if she doesn't answer, she'll find herself back under the tree.
>
> Stop!

Baba laughs. Nermin cries. Baba laughs even more. I am jig-jogging on his lap. I have no idea why he's laughing, but he's my father, so I repeat after him.

Nermin and I share a bedroom in Abu Dhabi and many times over in Cairo. We share a bedroom until she marries, and until then we fight like cats and dogs from home to home and room to room. While we do, our father moves from country to country chasing the buck. He tries his hand at a few jobs and cycles through failed business ventures with no luck, then comes back. When he comes back, I wait for him by the window, for his head and his bags to pop out of some car pulling up. Nermin and I fight like cats and dogs until one day it's my mother, Nermin, and me, and my father is puff, gone.

Cairo, 2000

He's in China now, so far from us, finally making it big, busy building an empire in the export business. He comes to Cairo from time to time with bags full of catalogs, product samples, and scraps of cloth. I wish for gifts, which he never brings, and yet I rummage through his bags, nevertheless. I search his suitcase once and find a photo in a picture frame. The photo is of a young Chinese woman carrying a baby girl. I ask him who they are. Is she his new wife? Is this his baby? But Baba lowers his gaze and slips from room to room.

The apartment on Orabi Street is bare except for the necessities. The ceramic floors are rug-less, the walls are naked, and there are no plants to tend. My mother, no longer daddy's girl nor any man's woman, goes to work to make a living, for us. She takes some basic computer skills courses and becomes a secretary in a business hotel by the pyramids.

Baba calls one day; he dials +2 02, he calls us.

Listen, I am getting old and I'm running a huge business here now. If I go, it goes with me unless you come and I show you the ropes.

Come where?

To China.

To China!

> If you come, it's going to be yours one day. If you don't, we lose it all. You'll have everything you want here.
>
> But Baba, I studied literature. I have nothing to do with business.
>
> Literature? What are you gonna do with that? Be a writer? Ha!

I go to China.

I go because where I'm from is not on the map, not anymore, so I seek the edges and overlook the borders. I go because I've inherited a gene that roams and the restless foot is mine to bear, too. The ghosts of the past are calling me, asking me to follow in their footsteps, to keep walking out and out. To stop is to know I am out of place, so I move from place to place. Perhaps in the farthest lands I might cease to feel like a stranger. Perhaps in leaving the world as he knows it, my father's finally found peace, so I follow. Two Palestinian renegades running toward the outpost, thinking we can leave ourselves behind. Thinking we can run until we vanish, with all our ghosts.

Shenzhen, 2000

China has more self-made female billionaires than any other country in the world. In fact, half of the world's wealthiest female billionaires are Chinese.

My father is about to introduce me to one of them. Ms. Xiuying Huijuan prevails over a global high-end handbag brand. There are four of us going to meet her: Talal, a Lebanese client living in Brazil, Hongxi, our Chinese interpreter, Baba, and me. Baba hits the top floor button in a glass elevator that overlooks the Shenzhen River, and we shoot up through a cool mist until the river disappears from sight.

The boardroom is a latex-white-on-latex-white vision of the future and my father seems intoxicated by the prospect of striking a lucrative deal. He's been raving about this woman for days, which makes me wonder, what makes her less *mara* than me. I hear her heels like a drumroll and they all stand, so I do too. She is tiny when she enters with an entourage, and she's wearing an all-white two-piece designer suit. My daughter, Baba says proudly, pointing at me. I step forward and she greets me with a hard handshake, then takes her place at the head of the table. We all sit down. Baba is slouched in a Made in China Tommy Hilfiger windbreaker double his size. He turns his gaze down. The door opens and Ms. Huijuan's staff brings in a collection of designer bags for our viewing. The bags are beautiful, wrapped in tissue, placed in boxes, tied in ribbons, slipped in posh pouches. In my notepad, I judiciously write the date, her name, our client's name, and the brand name. Only soon after, I realize there are no notes to take really, just a show to sit back and watch.

There is a game that ancient Chinese politicians used to play. It's called Qu Shui Liu Shang, and it involves floating a full glass of wine down a shallow creek. Whoever is sitting where the glass lands must drink and write a poem. Today, the game is played across boardrooms in China to win deals and establish hierarchies of power. The idea is to use your silver tongue to drink your opponent under the table. If you can prove your eloquence, negotiating power, and trustworthiness after the umpteenth drink, then you preside over a deal or win a promotion.

I watch as Baijiu, a clear white spirit, is served. The coffee boy places a cup in front of me, but a sideway glance from my father tells me to stay out of this. Ms. Huijuan stands up and makes the first toast, the *ganbei* as they call it, or the dry glass. I continue to fiddle awkwardly with my pen as they all raise their glasses and shoot the first cup down. Ms. Huijuan slams her cup on the table and calls for Baba to go next, to make a toast, but he doesn't stand up or make a toast. He remains slouched in his seat and in monotone introduces his Lebanese client as a billionaire in his own right. I know how this game will go because I have witnessed his ways before.

When he lived with us back in Cairo, he and I would often play Monopoly. He would buy me out of every property from Old Kent Road to Mayfair then relentlessly tease me for losing until I broke down in tears. It didn't matter that I was a child, that I was his child, or that it was just a game. The thrill of winning trumped all. Now he's at it again. Never mind the traditional Chinese saying that when one drinks with a friend, a thousand cups are not enough. He's not here to make friends or play nice. He is here to win, his way, and fuck all else.

Ms. Huijuan takes note, and for the next three hours or so has one mission in mind: to drink my father under the table at any cost. I watch him steadily slam one cup after the other as she falters and her team drops out one after the other. But the woman is determined. She asks for the Shaoxing, the red rice wine, and the beer to drink between toasts, then moves our shrunken party to a smaller, all-glass room. They drink more and more and talk business less and less until her red Shaoxing spills on her white suit. My father takes this as a sign that the game is over. He stands up, and we all do too. She is slouched in her chair when he gives her ruddy hand a hard handshake.

Tell her we have a lot more to discuss, he tells Hongxi, let her people call me when she's ready. We have forty-eight hours in Shenzhen before we fly out.

Beirut, 1994

I am seventeen years old when I leave my mother in Cairo to reunite with the entire Serhan family in Beirut. The Lebanese Civil War has just ended, and my Palestinian clan descends on the city from all corners of the earth: from Saudi Arabia, Qatar, the UAE, and Jordan, and from Cyprus, the United Kingdom, and the United States.

Bullets on building façades expose abandoned war sites. Beirut windows are gaping holes that look into rooms ripped into two. Rubble, rust, and peeling paint line the streets, where big black dogs still prowl. But, Beirut has turned its ravaged buildings into nightclubs where everyone dances on tables to forget the scars of war.

I tag along to a taverna where the family orders everything on the menu and copious amounts of *arak*, a Mediterranean spirit made of anise. Araq clouds cups and minds fast, as I am about to learn. I am intimidated by this international set called my family. My male cousins are handsome and worldly. They've been sent to private boarding schools in the UK and universities in the United States. The girls are brazen and beautiful. They color their hair with Sun-In and have boyfriends called George and Jean-Michel who, behind our family's back, pick them up on motorcycles in the middle of the night. My uncles have an easy elegance about them. They sit back and smile while their glamorous wives cackle. The party is boisterous as they make toast after toast.

To Beirut!

Long live Lebanon!

To Palestine, one day!

I watch quietly, invisibly, and squirm as I sip the bitter-sweet drink. I've never tasted alcohol before. My father never allowed it, but he seems happy surrounded by all his family, exceptionally so. A few cups down and a sound finally comes out of me. I stand up and ask everybody to be quiet, shhhh, I have something to say. I am awkward and scrawny and no one's used to me initiating conversations. They stop to listen. I get up on the table, raise my cup, and knock the chandelier. My cup cracks. Baba is amused. He brings me another cup and pours me another drink. I take a sip and proceed to tell a joke in my Egyptian accent. The adults love my Egyptian accent. It conjures up the golden age of Egyptian cinema with its legends, such as Abdel Halim Hafez and Faten Hamama, and the glorious years of Pan-Arabism and Gamal Abdel Nasser. I am more than the sum of my parts to them right now.

Ssshh, listen. I'll tell you a joke: A mummy covered in chocolate has been discovered in Egypt.

Archeologists believe it may be Pharaoh Rocher.

I watch them laugh so hard they nearly fall off their chairs.

Nizar, your daughter is drunk!

On the way back to my aunt's apartment in Tallet al-Khayyat, Baba warns me not to tell my mother he let me drink. He tells me to lower my voice, but I'm neither listening nor walking straight. He carries my limp body on his shoulder five floors up to my aunt's apartment while I sing and sway my upside-down head of hair. Israeli missiles have slammed into the hills of Beirut recently, destroying two power stations and plunging the city into darkness, but Saudi Arabian billionaire Prince Al-Waleed bin Talal Al Saud says he will pay the full cost of rebuilding them. Until then, Baba has to walk up with me on his shoulder.

The next morning over a breakfast feast of all kinds of *manakeesh* and *knafeh*, Baba's heart is full from last night's communion. He summons all my cousins, my sister, and me to line up in front of him.

> When I call on you, he says, I want you to step forward and tell me your full names and where you're from.

When it's my turn, I step forward toward him and feel confused: I cannot tell whether the words rolling off my tongue are new or old, whether I'm lost or found.

> Mai Nizar Faris Nayef Mohamed Ali Kheir Serhan, I say, Palestinian from al-Kabri.

Baba, you taught me my name is lineage bound to land. That I am of a place I have never seen yet must always call by my name, but you did not really elaborate on any of it. We had horse stables and a wine cellar, you once said to me as I followed you from room to room, your eyes lowered, avoiding my gaze. Perhaps the rest of the story was a scream stuck in your throat or locked up in a black box. Whatever it was, it led me to assume horse stables and a wine cellar was all there was to it.

Cairo, 1916

Zeinab Hanem Anis is my maternal great-grandmother, Hanem being an aristocratic Ottoman title conferred on women of noble descent. She and her sisters were educated and groomed in Circassia and Turkey during the Ottoman rule, which controlled Southeastern Europe, Western Asia, and North Africa between the fourteenth and early twentieth century. In 1916, the primed sisters were sent to Egypt to marry into wealthy families. Zeinab Hanem Anis married Mustafa Bey Salama, Bey being an honorary Ottoman title equivalent to "sir" in English. She lived in Cairo and was a writer, signing off with the pen name "Sina," which is her family name, Anis, written backward. Zeinab Hanem also hosted a cultural salon at her home, which now, more than a century later, is the French Cultural Center in the Mounira neighborhood of Cairo.

Zeinab Hanem and Mustafa Bey had five children together: Shayanne, the eldest daughter, then Mohsen, Camelia, and Isis, and finally, their youngest son, Anis. Family legend has it that on the occasion of the birth of Anis, Egyptian Prime Minister Mustafa al-Nahhas Basha paid the family a home visit. Zeinab Hanem was ill at the time, having just given birth, and bed rest was advised. Yet, this was no ordinary guest. Despite feeling weak, the lady pulled herself out of bed, dressed to the nines, and went out into the garden to receive her special guest. Zeinab Hanem died a few days later of childbed fever, a postpartum infection of the reproductive tract.

Following her death, the children scattered, forming a little diaspora of their own amongst other relatives in other homes and other neighborhoods. Mustafa Bey Salama would ride his black horse down the streets of Cairo in a state of mournful stupor, stopping at one brothel after another, where he would tie his horse's reigns to the trees. He died shortly after, too, of a broken heart.

In a black-and-white photo in my possession, Zeinab Hanem Anis sits in a lace dress with leather riding boots peeping out from beneath its hem. Her siblings all stand around her. Her youngest brother is blonde under a tarbouche. Her sisters both have their hair up in chignons. Zeinab Hanem's hair is tied in a long and thick braid down to her cinched waist. She is a sight to behold in a wealth of dainty fabric—delicious, desirous, like layers upon layers of crumbly pastry, her eyes fixing the camera with both merriment and mystery. She almost fools me into believing she is looking at me, that I can reach out and bridge the hundred-year gap, touch all that life force, her hand.

Cairo, 1985

Cars, cars are unsafe spaces. I am seven years old in the passenger seat of my father's car. He is driving down El Nile Street when I make some silly remark. It enrages him. He opens my door, forces me out, and drives off. Without warning, it is just me and the streets. I stare at the chaos, the shapeless crowd, the endless traffic. People are packed in microbuses like sardines in cans, people on motorcycles are mounting the sidewalks to bypass traffic, a horse dragging a cart can't take the load anymore and collapses on the asphalt. I think of Nermin: We found you under a tree, I am not your real dad, and I begin to cry. Through my tears I spot his car coming back, I spot his face. He's U-turned to get me, and he's laughing. He finds it all hilarious.

Cairo, 1985

Cars, cars are dangerous spaces with my father at the steering wheel. He's there now with my mother next to him and me and my sister in the back seat. I watch them fight, I watch my mother weep. I press my forehead against the cold window and drift. The only thing I see in my reflection is one iris like a dark well. The rest of my face is smudged with lights, the red and yellow from the cars outside. Suddenly, a car comes speeding toward us from a side street. It comes dangerously close, almost grazes our car, then overtakes, and all hell breaks loose. Our car is a death wish that skids and screeches. Horns all around us sound off, and the car fills with screams.

Crying is ridiculous, I tell myself.

Acre, 1897

You were not always a renegade, Baba. You deny yourself your resplendent roots.

Own them.

Your great grandfather, Mohamed Serhan: In 1897, having attended the salons and coteries of learning and the French missionary schools of Istanbul, he returned to the Palestinian town of Safad where he joined the Ottoman Empire's imperial treasury in charge of managing imperial revenues. Mohamed Serhan climbed steady up this career ladder to eventually become the treasurer of both Safad and Acre. Soon after, the Ottomans bestowed upon him the noble title of effendi.

One day, as the mustachioed effendi trotted on a black horse along the lush roads of Acre, he spotted a beautiful young woman, and, in a flash, was besotted. The woman was Khashfa Balqis, daughter of a wealthy landowner from al-Kabri, and soon to be your great-grandmother. It is said that Mohamed loved Khashfa so much that he left Safad and planted his roots in al-Kabri to be by her side. In these fertile farmlands, the original patriarch obtained an Ottoman decree to use Ayn Kabri and Ayn al-'Asal to tend his land. He ploughed endless fields, olive groves, and citrus orchards, dug wells, erected mills, set up oil presses, stocked warehouses full of grains, bred cattle, opened al-Kabri's first school, built the family's first stronghold, bore five children, and established himself as a beacon of popular and political leadership in the north of Palestine.

Atef Serhan, Mohamed's eldest son: He had some great shoes to fill, and he did fill them at a challenging time. He expanded the family's wealth and influence as eighteen thousand Jewish immigrants arrived on streamliners in 1921 and while the British purchased land on behalf of the Jewish National Fund from rich Arabs who vacationed in Palestine. With the need for a popular front becoming more pressing, Atef Serhan established the first grand divan, a council for religious, tribal, and political leaders as well as intellectuals and administrators. They met regularly to deliberate on matters of mobilization, resistance, and liberation. They formed alliances, took action, moved masses. People went on strike, stopped paying taxes, revolted, they took up arms.

Atef's brother, Nayef Serhan, your grandfather: He built a house for his son, your father, Faris Serhan, one they say he paid for in 24-karat gold.

Faris Serhan, your father: He campaigned tirelessly against British and Jewish land purchases in Palestine. He joined the Arab Palestinian Conference in 1927, the Bloudan Conference in 1937, and the Arab Higher Committee in 1948. Don't believe them, Baba, when they tell you that you sold your land. I'll tell you who did. On August 19, 1935, a company was founded in Beirut to specifically sell land in the South of Lebanon and Palestine. The founders were then-Prime Minister Khayr al-Din al-Ahdab, Wasfi al-Din Qadura, Joseph Khadij, Michel Sarji, Mourad Danna, and Elias al-Haj. There were individuals from other Lebanese families as

31

well, like Youssef, Naguib, and George of the renowned Sursok family. They sold 9,884 acres of Palestinian land. Al-Sallam sold 40,772 acres. Antoine and Michel of the al-Tiyan family sold 76,108 acres, al-Twayni sold the Ibn Amer pastures and lands between Acre and Haifa, al-Sabbagh sold coastal land, al-Kjour sold 951 acres, and al-Kabbani sold 988 acres. Wealthy Syrian families sold your land, too. Al-Youssef sold land in al-Butayha and al-Zawiya in Safad. Al-Mardini, al-Qutli, al-Gazayri, al-Shama'a, and al-Emari all sold your land for big money. They offered extortionate amounts to buy land in their names only to transfer the property titles to the British and in turn to the Jewish National Fund.[2]

I am not making this up, Baba; it's all online, but I also have a letter. It was passed down to me by your sister, Nadia. The letter is from Faris Serhan, written in his own handwriting and dated 1936. I have it laminated and tucked away on a bookshelf where no one can touch it. It details all this and more. You never sold your land, Baba. No Palestinian did. Ours was our pride, our pleasure; the land of plenty, and there was enough to go around. When al-Gishis grew apples in their orchards and al-Qadis grew figs in theirs, they would gift each other baskets full of love and fruit. All the money in the world was simply not worth losing it.

Cairo, 1928

With the early deaths of Zeinab Hanem Anis and Mustafa Bey Salama, their children were dispersed among various Anis and Salama households. Mohsen, Camelia, and Shayanne were sent to their Egyptian father's side of the family. Isis and Anis were sent to their Circassian mother's side. The inheritance, however, remained in the iron grip of their paternal aunt long after the children had come of age.

The children had varied upbringings. The ones who ended up in Egyptian households grew up more conservatively, more traditionally, even more provincially, in homes where men had handlebar mustaches and were proper Egyptian patriarchs. Isis and Anis, however, grew up in homes that were multi-cultured, with ladders for the bookshelves and many languages heard around the house. Yet the underlying sentiment shared among all siblings was one: They were disenfranchised of home and land. They did not belong.

Guangzhou, 2000

In Guangzhou, Hongxi and I speak to each other in Arabic *fusha*, since he doesn't understand my Egyptian dialect and I don't understand Cantonese. He kindly offers to teach me basic words so that I can get by: transactional terms, numbers from one to ten, *hello*, 你好, *how much*, 多少, and *thank you*, 谢谢你. I write it all down in my notepad. At the entrance of The Canton Import and Export Fair, Baba tasks me with introducing our business to suppliers in sixteen categories. We then split, Hongxi goes with Baba, and I go it alone.

In the toy zone, I say 你好 to a man behind a desk and point to myself, I am Mai. He sits back in his chair, squints at me, and leans forward. He takes off his glasses, tries to rearrange my parts so I can make sense. I give him Baba's business card. He turns it around in his hand. He seems not to understand what it is, as if it might be anything other than what it is.

We are an export company, I say in English, and this is our business card. I wait for him to say anything, but he seems to have run out of words, out of ideas for what to make of me. I spot a pack of his business cards on the desk and grab one quickly. May I, I ask, and get up. He doesn't answer.

謝謝, I say, bowing.

I walk over to the zone for medical devices, the vehicles and spare parts, the electronics, the household appliances, the chemical products, where the same scenario repeats itself over and over again. Everyone seems to think I am some strange and bewildering apparition. I go from Mai, to Mia, to M謝a, and begin to feel woozy. Fuck this shit, is all I want to say. I simply cannot go back to Baba with nothing to show but this story. He's going to think it's because of me, because I'm dangerous cargo, extra baggage, a discomfort, a *mara*. Baba would hate this story.

Cars are dangerous places with my father at the steering wheel, but put him in the back seat and you're in for an equally adverse reaction. He likes to be in control, and if he isn't, he loses all control. In a car in China, he cannot be in control, because he's being driven around everywhere.

He dismisses Hongxi for the day and instructs him to return later for a business dinner, then hails a taxi in front of The Canton Import and Export Fair. He tells the driver to head to our hotel, Langham Place, five minutes away. The driver takes the long route, adding sixteen more minutes to the trip and fare. He drives up the Huanan Expressway and hits traffic over the Zheijiang River, into the Tianhe District, and up again on the Guangyuan Expressway.

Mai, Baba says, this driver has taken the long route. Why?

He thinks we're tourists.

Tell him then, I say.

Baba says nothing. We enter Huizhan E Road, where our hotel is located, and get off by the entrance. Baba gives the driver half the fare. The man objects, flails his arms, shouts in Cantonese. Baba slips his hand into the narrow window opening, grabs the driver by the lapel, and wraps it around his wrist. Before I know it, he is banging the driver's limp body against the car window. There's a cigarette dangling from Baba's mouth. With every bang, more cherries fall off and form holes in his shirt.

Night falls and I'm spent. I do not want to risk Baba's wrath, but my inability to speak my mind following the incident with the driver is filling me with rage. I think of ordering a burger from the hotel's international menu, maybe a burger will soothe me, when Baba asks if I'm up for eating in a halal restaurant.

What do you say?

Maybe?

Okay, but you should know, he tells me, it's different.

What do you mean, different?

You'll see.

He makes some calls and soon we are accompanied by Hongxi, and an an all-male entourage complete with potbellies, comb-overs, and macho vibes, from resident Syrian traders and Jordanian agents to Lebanese and Palestinian visiting businessmen—and me.

Baba takes us through the beat-up backstreets of Guangzhou behind the silver-lit façade. The alleyways here are dark and slithery with musty walls and decaying drainage pipes that spill sewage along our path. I sidestep auto rickshaws that zigzag through rainbow-tinted puddles. I bump into veiled women with dry hands. We're just around the corner from the wannabe-models who strut their stuff along the towering glass of the high street, but none of that new money seems to have ended up here.

We enter a restaurant with an aluminum-framed door and window decals reading, *Halal*, in red and green.

Whatever you do, Baba says, don't use the toilet or look inside the kitchen.

Why?

He doesn't answer. I take my seat on a wobbly wooden table for six covered in a stained oilcloth. The men all squeeze next to Baba on one side, with the exception of Hongxi. He sits next to me, then quickly realizes he might have broken some social code, and squeezes next to the men on the other side of the table. I am hoping for a familiar taste, shish taouk with vegetables or a beef hotpot, but sticky rice and string beans are the only food items I can decipher on the menu. I eat quietly, invisibly, while the men discuss business and smoke cigarettes. I try to ignore the crowd forming outside the restaurant. They've spotted me and are calling their children, shopkeepers, neighbors, and friends to come look.

Then they open the restaurant door and push a woman in. She comes to our table with a camera and gestures to me to come out and take a picture with everyone. I look at all the men at my table, who have been straining to avoid me so far. They double down on discomfort. I push my chair out and accompany the woman to the street. Outside, I squat in the center while more and more people squeeze into the frame.

After dinner, Baba takes me to see a woman called Lin. He's hyped about seeing her, about introducing her to me. She's his friend, he says with a twinkle. She's built an impressive fashion business from the ground up. She is beautiful. She is a work machine. She is boss. I compute from all of that that she might be a little more than what Baba is willing to reveal.

Our car pulls up to a wholesale marketplace near Beijing Road. The area is packed with all kinds of merchandise, negotiation, rattle. Lin waits in front of her shop with a group of young women. I know who she is before we get out of the car. There is no power suit in sight, no frills. She's beautiful anyway in her white t-shirt, blue jeans, long pony tail. She is a quiet force, I note, in that comfortable-in-one's-own-skin sort of way.

Her all-female crew seem very happy to see Baba. He seems to be popular with the women here, and I wonder, am I the only one who sees him as a shriveled Arab man with a bald head and an oversized jacket? He doesn't even speak their language. He's beaming though from ear to ear, basking in all the attention. Lin stands behind her all-female team, eyes fixed on Baba with affection. She is waiting for the women's excitement to subside so her turn to greet him comes. Baba gives her an uncharacteristic hug.

At the steps leading up to her shop, I spot a group of men sitting down before a tray filled with empty porcelain cups of green tea and cans of black beer. They chat and people-watch while their kids run around their feet. I walk up, past their stares.

Lin leads us up to the second floor. There are more women here, women by sewing machines, by pattern-cutting tables, poring over accounts, making inventory. We take our place around a long rectangular table. Boxes arrive, scotch-taped and labeled. Lin unhooks a key chain from her belt loop and flicks open a fake Swiss knife. She slits the boxes open and brings out the merchandise. She flicks her long ponytail over her shoulder. What follows is not so much a business negotiation but a flirtatious dance. Baba only has eyes for Lin. He speaks softly to her, he cannot seem to help it, and for once all his hidden strife dissipates.

Acre, pre-1948

Baba, did you ever wonder why al-Kabri smelt like iodine even though the sea was fifteen kilometers away to the west? I'll tell you why, there was nothing to obstruct the wind's movement. The mountains and the breeze could both exist. The mountains would fade at sunset and blend in with the colors of the sky, orange and lavender. The water, fifty meters below land, flowed freely from coast to springs, all the way down under the land's skin, coloring it in bronze and green tones.

It's all under your skin, I know that too. I know your body parts are the coast, cliffs, valleys and wide plains of your village, and why they too will stop breathing soon. Why you'll stop running, why your body will break. It will no longer be able to break sugar. You burn a hundred cigarettes a day, Baba; you burn the tobacco fields over the hills every day. But I also know our bloodline, our bloodline is like a tree in a storm, its branches break, they disband in the wind with nothing to obstruct their movement.

Cairo, 1984

Football is a sport embraced by all Egyptians. Boys make balls from scraps of old socks and pieces of sponge to play in all the alleyways. Men don't touch food or their wives for days if—God forbid—their team loses. Egyptian state media floods radio stations and television channels with patriotic songs before a match to deflect political unrest. When the game is on, Egyptians retreat to their living rooms, sit before their television sets, and the streets turn into a ghost town. The only sound one hears outside is the occasional uproar of those sitting upright before their screens.

It is one of those days when the two major Egyptian teams, Ahly and Zamalek, are competing for the Egyptian Premier League. My mother, Nermin, and I are Ahly supporters. We've always been. It runs in Mama's family. Baba though, he's at it again, being a renegade, rooting for Zamalek, just because. We huddle before our TV, like millions around the country, and the air is charged. Ahly scores a goal, Zamalek follows with another. Ahly scores a second goal and Zamalek follows with yet another. Ahly scores a third and final goal, and Nermin and I begin to bounce off the walls. We hug. We wave the Ahly flag from our window. We pierce the night with our uproar. Then Nermin gets up. She goes up to our father and sticks her tongue out. But our father can't handle losses, big or small. He cannot distinguish between big and small. Nermin is small and he is big. When his hand lands on her face, she falls to the floor.

Outside our window, cars begin to flood the streets. Millions of Egyptians are celebrating tonight, and the other half won't touch food, won't touch their wives. As for us, the party disbands suddenly and the lights go off. I try to sleep, but Nermin's curled-up back is keeping me awake. She's not moving, but I know her eyes are wide open in the dark. I mutter her name, but she doesn't answer. I hear our parents argue and I get up, tiptoe towards the strife. The door to their room is open. Their silhouettes are two meters apart. I hold my breath.

Cairo, 1988

Grief and loss show up in one's body to warn, to say that this is no way to live. Body cells bereaved can no longer bear it, can no longer taste or break sugar.

That day in 1988, Baba took the family out for lunch, and in a packed restaurant leaned forward and spoke softly. He spoke to my mother like there was no one else in the room. I have diabetes, is all I heard. I did not know what diabetes was, but I remember how the air suddenly turned thick, how his eyes were searching hers for a lost love to emerge, or pity that might perhaps lead to reparation. That man, once tall and strong with a huge appetite, a man who used to eat everything with Arabic bread, even rice, seemed shrunken as he chewed on a cigarette and fiddled with yellow-stained fingers.

P

A

L

E

S

T

I

N

I

A

N

diaspora: dots on a Where We Fly airline map. Each dot is a city and hundreds of thousands of me, give or take, because no one is keeping count. The world's hot and slick future is numeric, but I'm an anomaly, because the future is innumerate when it comes to me.

So I fly and do what I've always done, seek asylums and wait for wars to end, when all the time war is inside me. While I wait, I adopt a home or it adopts me and I live while other lives live within me. Eventually, I blend in, I become a moth on sandstone or a hare in the snow, until a beady eye turns and calls me out.

> Who are you?
> Mai.
> Mai who?
> Serhan.
> Sarhan?
> Ser— it's fine, it's a small difference.
> Huh?
> I'm Palestinian.
> Oh.

Cairo, 1969

Nana barely knew the groom when he came to ask for her hand in marriage. Neither did her mother, Isis. So little did Isis know that in order to welcome him and his family, she prepared a lavish seafood feast.

Nizar walked in, tall legs in bell bottoms, his pompadour waxed brilliantly. He sat down, inhaling the fishy sea trail that escaped the kitchen door, and, within minutes, felt queasy. His skin blotched and his eyes clouded like dead fish. Nizar could not breathe, and everyone panicked. They called a doctor. As it turned out, he was severely allergic to seafood.

Cairo, 1990

Baba hates cats, and yet in the apartment on Orabi Street, we have three. We usually feed them dry food, but sometimes, when we run out and Baba isn't around, we open a can of tuna.

We run out of dry food one day, we run out while Baba's out. We open a tuna can and the cats eat, filling their little bellies with flakes of fish. When Baba returns home, he detects trails of the fishy smell instantly. Turning a shade of blood, he picks up one cat and flings it across the room. Home splits. Everywhere is scared.

Cairo, 1985

Little me is a silence, and silence is a violence severing me from my surroundings. In and out of the frame, my world wars before me, and around. Sometimes, I will say something. I will throw a word out into a car or a house and hide, watch its flames lick everything.

It's okay to self-soothe when I'm small, but growing up isn't easy, so I continue to suck my thumb. I suck it in cupboards, under tables, and behind closed doors, but my mother still knows. I am three years old, I am five then six, and still suck my thumb. My mother tries everything to help me kick my habit. She gives me a teddy bear to hug, drowns my thumb in a nasty-tasting oil, but my world won't stop warring, so why should I stop sucking my thumb?

My parents send me to school so that they fight in private, and I'm getting nervous in class. I sit in the back row hoping to hide, but attendance sheets call me out. All the other kids are rowdy, they're all over the place, but they must stay in their seats. The religion teacher, Mr. Saeed, he's in a silk shirt with silver threading and a mustache, glossed and trimmed. He walks slowly up and down the aisles, arms crossed behind him:

Today is Quran recital day. You will recite verses 1–50 from Surat an-Nisa'. I hope you learnt it by heart, because if you didn't—

He stops, turns his beady eyes on us and calls the first name, then the second and third in no particular order. It's a game of Russian Roulette and I can see all the heads dunk a little. The girl with a long brown ponytail gets up and recites something about fear, women, two or three or four wives. I raise my hand. Mr. Saeed, I need the toilet, I say, and inside that toilet booth I take a minute or three or four to suck my thumb.

I'm seven years old, I'm eight and still have not kicked the habit. The kids in school catch me sucking. That boy, Hussein, I'll never forget his name, crawls under the table and finds me there. He finds it funny.

Limassol, 1990

I forget the happy places. My cousins and me descending from all corners of the earth on a pretty beach town. My Teta's apartment on Tzon Kennedy Street with broad balconies and sea views for every room. Three months of sun, sea, and summer. My uncles' wives telling their daughters to tuck their tummies in their bikinis as the whole tribe flocks along the Panagies coast. The pedestrian walkway at sunset, its candied apples, corn cobs, and arcades. My cousin Fadi carving the watermelon heart, the sweetest part, just for himself. Us girls slipping into miniskirts, waiting for Teta to finish her game of cards and retire to bed so we can all sneak out and hit the pizzerias, ice-cream parlors, and discotheques.

At night, coming back bare foot, singing *Another Day in Paradise*. Missing lunch the next day at noon because we're all zonked out until one. That sunny Palestinian kitchen always ready, always packed with women, their heaves and shrieks and strong hands and flawless skin. Each table and countertop a work station with an aunt or an aunt's aunt rubbing lamb chop with spice or rinsing luscious fruit. Those Cypriot cherries, more carmine than any cherry I've ever seen.

They say memory imagines. Every time it summons the past, it merely summons the gist of it and layers it with acquired stories we pick up along the way. Maybe I don't remember that happy place because so much has happened since, so much has changed.

I was too young to understand that there was a civil war in Lebanon at that time; I found that out later. The reason why my Teta fled to Cyprus in the first place. She waited for the war to end there for fourteen years, until graffiti started to show up on the walls: Don't Sell Cyprus to the Lebanese. Yes, we were considered Lebanese by then. Jeddo Abu Saleh, my great-grandfather, he was there too, sitting on his bedroom balcony, a fossil of his village. My grandfather must've been there too, but I don't remember him, and now I know why—because no one wanted to remember who he once was, because by now he had been robbed of all of it.

Cairo, 1941

The Circassian homes of the Anis clan were warm and caring, but Isis and Anis Salama never felt at home. Being the youngest of all five orphans meant that they had experienced the wild long before knowing what home is, and once wild, one cannot domesticate.

My grandmother Isis fell in love with my grandfather Mohey, a law student outside her social milieu. Her guardians rejected him. He was middle-class, God forbid. The blonde, fair-skinned Isis ran off with him anyway. At sixteen, she forged her age on their marriage certificate, bumping it up to eighteen. Nothing was going to get in the way of her marrying the man who made her wild heart thump, not even her brother Mohsen. Nothing was going to stop Mohsen from trying to stop her, either. With eyes as ice-blue as a Husky's and a mustache of splendid honey tones, he could not conceive of his sister running off with "a riff-raff." He secured a pistol and threatened to kill them both. For years he parked himself under their modest love nest with fire in his pocket, to no avail.

As for Anis, he grew up watching Mohsen switch cars and women from moon to moon. He grew up wanting his share of his parents' inheritance, his legal right. He wanted to travel, to leave Egypt, to carve a new life for himself abroad. It wasn't going to be an easy battle,

not with Mohsen being the eldest, the sole benefactor—
but nothing was going to get in the way of Anis either.
At seventeen, he paid Mohsen a visit in his office. He
rolled up his sleeves, snapped his suspenders, and raised
his fists in the air.

Do not play this game with me, he warned, I'm not
a pushover. I'll fight you if need be.

Cairo, 1986

Mr. Egbert is our school music teacher. He teaches us all
the songs of famous musicals: *My Fair Lady*, *Phantom of
the Opera*, and *Joseph and the Amazing Technicolor Dreamcoat*.
He assigns the students with good voices solo parts, and
the rest join the chorus while he plays the piano. I've
never seen a teacher more consumed with the love of his
subject than Mr. Egbert. He begins every song sitting up
straight and poised, then things take a wild turn.

As he hits the keys and our voices rise, finding har-
mony, the veins on Mr. Egbert's hands begin to bulge.
Slowly, he stands up, and his face turns an amazing
Technicolor, too. I watch him bang and bang on the
piano in a climactic trance until a little bulge begins to
expand in his pants, too.

He's at it again today. He's enjoying the song "Close
Every Door to Me" from *Joseph and the Amazing Technicolor
Dreamcoat*. It's a sad but beautiful song about the Israelites,
a people who roam without a land, who have been prom-
ised a land of their own. It touches a chord within me,
and I sing it on repeat all day, in school, on the bus, I belt
it out like no one's listening, at home.

But someone is listening alright. It's Baba. He drops what he's doing and storms into my bedroom. For a second there, I think he is about to smack me, so I hide my head between my knees.

What is this? What are you singing?

It's from *Joseph and the Amazing Technicolor Dreamcoat*, I tell him, isn't it beautiful?

Mashallah. I pay premium tuition for this private school. For what? For this!

The next day my father asks for a meeting with the school principal.

I'm only nine years old; I know next to nothing about history or politics. All I see is images of war on the TV screen at home every night. That only means one thing to me—that I often don't get to watch the cartoon channels I want to watch.

I tell a friend in school about the incident with the song and how it enraged my father.

Maybe Mr. Egbert is a Jew, my friend tells me.

Oh.

You want to test it?

How?

Draw a swastika on your forehead next time you're in class and see how Mr. Egbert reacts.

I think it's all fun and games and want more kids in on it. The next week, I tell everyone in class to draw a swastika on their foreheads too. We all enter the music room and wait for Mr. Egbert to notice.

What is this? Who started this?

The other kids all burst out laughing and point at me. I'm in trouble. I know that because Mr. Egbert's face is turning Technicolor once again. He storms out of class and asks me to follow.

In the corridors of school, he cracks his knuckles, clears his throat, before introducing me to a man called Adolf Hitler and the story of the Holocaust.

I am sorry, I say, holding back the tears.

Beirut, 1995

I fly into Beirut from Cairo and Teta makes my favorites: rolled vine leaves, zucchini stuffed with rice and lamb, and *kibbeh bel laban*. Baba rolls up his sleeves to eat and finds no yoghurt to dip his food in. He asks me to run down and buy some *laban*. I run down and I come back with a bottle of milk. Baba gets angry, so angry.

Laban means *yoghurt*, *halib* means *milk*, he says, banging the glass bottle on the table. But I do not know that. I live in Egypt, I speak Egyptian, and in fucking Egyptian, *laban* means *milk*.

China, 2000

Working long hours is an unwritten rule in China, and my father has lived here so long that this work ethic now defines him, too. In fact, he has more reason to persist over hardship, to work through exhaustion. If he stops, he will see what his ghost looks like, so he never stops.

He's relentless.

Every day a different town or province, on flights that whisk us from chilling winter to monsoon summer; new clients, factories, board rooms, markets, warehouses, around-the-clock meetings and late-night negotiations, sleepless nights in five-star hotels, office apartments, endless green mountains on the road, and everywhere an entourage. Cha-ching, cha-ching is the only sound he hears, and every move, every mile, is calculated to rake in more.

Wuhan, 2000

After Guangzhou, Baba, Hongxi, and I fly to Wuhan and check into the Westin Hotel. I've been following him around since 6 a.m. when we boarded that plane. His client here is a Lebanese businessman living in Chile, a tycoon of the textile business, and Baba is fired up. We go from airport to hotel, from hotel to factory, from factory to office, from office to warehouse, and from warehouse to marketplace. At 10 p.m., Baba wants to take the meeting to our hotel reception, and that is when I bow out. I just can't.

At 2 a.m., I wake up to a knock on the door. I open and it is him, arms draped on Hongxi's shoulders, head slumped, eyes closed. He's overworked, and he's fainted.

Hongxi lays him in bed and helps me take off his jacket and eye glasses. I put his keys and a bundle of cash bound in an elastic band on the bedside table. I straighten his body in bed, make him comfortable. I take off his shoes and his socks. I notice that the skin on his right foot is moist and turning a yellowish grey. I notice Hongxi turning blue in the face. The stench of rot filling up the room is unbearable, and soon I turn blue too. Hongxi points at his foot.

他的脚, he mumbles, *qadamu*.

Yiwu, 2000

Baba and I catch a flight two days later to Yiwu and Hongxi flies back to Shenzhen to attend to more business. Although Baba has an apartment here, we stay in the Shangri-La Hotel, a few minutes from the small commodities market, and leave the apartment to his Yiwu assistant, Ou.

Ou is introduced to me in the hotel lobby on a rainy day. She's different. Unlike the giggly women who fawn over my father in other towns, she's stone-faced. Her flared lip, though, betrays her, forming a sensuous hole in her impenetrable front.

We head to the restaurant where I order a filet mignon from the international menu and she orders tofu and steamed rice. I observe the way Ou eats. She has a carnivorous way of eating non-carnivorous things, almost predatory, and beads of sweat billow on her forehead. When she speaks, though, it is only in whispers, in Baba's ear. Something about that rubs me the wrong way, and I speak to him in Arabic so she doesn't understand. I state the obvious, that it's pouring rain outside. My socks are soaked inside my sneakers, and I do not have a jacket or umbrella. I desperately need winter clothes. He tells Ou to finish her lunch and take me shopping.

Ou and I split from my father to go shopping. She walks in front of me on the high street. Every time I try to catch up with her, she picks up her pace. We walk into a shop, and I begin to look through the racks, but she has her arms folded on her chest and her shoe won't stop tapping the floor.

Ou, I don't think you want to be here.

No, I don't, she says.

That's alright, you don't have to. Just give me the hotel business card. I will finish and come back on my own.

She hands me the business card and, without saying goodbye, leaves.

I walk in and out of shops buying what I need and then try to hail a taxi, but no one is willing to take me. Drivers look at the address on the business card and drive off without an explanation. An hour passes and I am ambushed once again by curious bodies and ogling eyes. I see them call their shopkeepers, friends, and neighbors. *Come! Check out this strange-looking girl. A foreigner!* I am drenched in rain and about to collapse when I hand one of the gawking men the business card in my hand. They all gather around him while the card gets passed from hand to hand. There is a big discussion around the address, one I do not understand. I wait until the shop metal doors roll down and I still do not understand. Finally, a man in an auto rickshaw waves at me to hop in.

I ride behind him on the auto rickshaw with no questions asked. He drives and drives through the night. He drives past closed shops and over highways, under bridges and across glistening expressways. I do not recall the distance being this far, the time being this long. Suddenly, we arrive at a toll station and drive through that too. I wonder if I am in a different town or a different province altogether. I have no idea. The highways are wide and the mountains on either side are neon-green and grand in the dark. There are no vehicles on the road, big or small, just this man and me on a wheezing auto rickshaw. I cannot communicate my worry to him, so it multiplies. The thought of being kidnapped takes hold of me. Not exactly the religious type, I hang on to the only thread left, prayer:

> *In the name of Allah the beneficent, the merciful. Praise be to the world's Lord. Beneficent, merciful, owner of the day of judgment. Thee alone we worship, Thee alone we ask for help. Show us the straight path.*

The hours eventually dwindle into minutes. We hit a busy town and I'm a born-again believer. *Hamdulillah,* I mumble under my breath. We get stuck in traffic and I am joyous. I spot the Shangri-La Hotel's glitzy façade. My driver drives up the ramp where I spot Baba. He has both hands on his hips and his face is the color of burning coal. I jump out of the auto rickshaw.

> It's Ou who did this, Baba. She left me there. She wanted me to get lost.

He wants to hit me. I can see the rage travel through his body, toward his hands.

> Are you listening to me? Your daughter was abandoned. That *bitch*, she didn't tell me we drove to another town. She knew I'd get lost and she still left me.

> Shut up, he says.

> She left me, on purpose, Baba, you have to do something. Fire her!

Acre, pre-1948

You never liked school, Baba. Maybe because the house in al-Kabri was home, you preferred to stay there. Your mother would go around chitchatting with all the household's working women, the ones filling the barrels with rainwater and the ones boiling the bay leaf. The ones tending the cinchona trees and the ones grating the oranges.

Your brothers all went to school without a fuss. Your sister, Nadia, did so well in her studies that your father sent her to Jerusalem to attend the exclusive Schmidt's Girls College, where she learned German and English. But you, every day at 7:30 a.m., the same scene. You would lie supine on the floor like dead weight. Your father would try to lift you up, and he would fail.

You will go to school, he would say.

I won't.

He would pull you by the arm, by the ear.

Why not?

I don't want to.

Why not!

It gives me a headache.

Your father, an effendi, son of an effendi, son of an effendi could not wrap his head around the idea of an uneducated son. What was even more troubling to him was that you, a little boy, could get your own way with him.

I put your photos next to his, Baba, and I know why you could get away with it: because you looked exactly like him. The only differences were his mustache and tarbouche. With him you got your way because you were his shadow, long and dark ahead of him. Beyond that land, those years, were the unknown streets where you would roam toward a point of no return. He saw it in you, and it frightened him.

Yiwu, 2000

I wake up in Yiwu feeling like I always do: hungry. I'm sick of the fava beans and hummus cans Arab clients bring my father from Syria, Lebanon, and Egypt. I miss food cooked with loving and familiar hands, food that tastes of home and not of mileage or time zones.

Eventually, I discover the fast-food chains, little pockets of Americana that oddly feel like home to me, maybe because they connect me with an outside world, wherever that may be. In the KFCs and McDonalds of China's southeast, I sit alone for breakfast, lunch, and dinner, scan people while they scan me, try against all odds to spot a friend or a family member in other people's features or gaits. They distract me from the chicken. It's dawning on me that something is not quite right with it, that it's probably not halal. I break the nugget into two and the flesh is a grayish white mottled in purple. It reminds me of my father's foot. I need to speak to him about going to see a doctor. I smother the nuggets with barbeque sauce to thwart the thought.

Baba, however, he's totally okay with canned food, coffee, and cigarettes. I walk through Yiwu's Chi'an town with him one day, across Dragon Creek and up the leafy Guyue Bridge. I notice the creek is so crystal clear that the reflection of the bridge forms a circle like a laurel wreath, then I notice he's starting to limp. But he has other things in mind. He wants to talk to me. We stop on the bridge, and while I take the scene in, he lights a cigarette.

You know, Mai, I came here in 1992. I had no money, I knew no one. Bought a map, rented a bicycle, and that is how it all began.

I nod.

What?

Good, I say.

That's all you got to say?

Very good?

Very good?

Well, what do you want me to say? You've made all this money and you don't even spend it.

Very good you say that, because it's what I want to talk to you about.

He puts an arm around my shoulder as if to put more weight on what he's about to say.

What is it with you and spending money, he asks.

What else are you meant to do with it?

Look at me, I'm a man of simple needs. All I need is my coffee and cigarettes.

I look at his worn-out leather shoes, his tacky bum bag, his fingers dried and stained like timeworn paper. I breathe in his ashes.

You could work much less for coffee and cigarettes, Baba.

Material things, that's all you care about, Mai.

That is not true. I came here to help you, to be with you.

The world is a transient place.

You are saying this, to me?

You're not taking any of it with you.

No, you listen to me, you are the one who is not taking any of this with you. You're wasting away here. You need to go back to Beirut and be around your family. You need to see a doctor.

He looks at me like he would a stranger then walks off down the bridge.

Baba? Baba!

I am not leaving this place, he says.

We lay in two single beds that night, and I cannot breathe. His right foot is swollen, in a terrifying scarlet color, and the nails are hard as tusks with visible ridges. I notice a blister around his ankle, then the stench pervades the room. I try to open the windows, but they're not the kind that open, and I feel trapped.

I call +2 02, I call Cairo, Mama. She tells me she misses me and I tell her I do, too. Baba sits up to listen, he hangs on to every word I say, tries to read between the lines, make out what she is saying to me. He waits for her to ask to speak to him, but she doesn't. Instead, she passes the phone to Nermin, but my conversation with Nermin is clipped. I can't talk when I can't breathe, and she doesn't want to talk knowing he's next to me, listening.

Give me the phone, he says, I want to speak to her.

Baba wants to speak to you, I tell her.

There's a silence on her end, and I can feel a darkness take hold of Nermin worlds away.

No, she says.

I hang up.

Why did you hang up? he asks.

She doesn't want to speak to you.

He slides down in bed and stares at the ceiling.

Your foot, Baba, you should get it checked.

Turn the lights off, he says.

I put the pillow on my head, but it does nothing to stop the stench from burning my nostrils. It does nothing to help with the sound. He's weeping.

He would like to buy Nermin a new car, he says in the dark. He would like to buy her a beach house on the Red Sea.

It's too late now, though.

Cairo, 1982

There is a proverb in Egypt that likens people to peacocks. To describe a proud and pompous person, you say, you're like a peacock, with a feather on your head.

I call my maternal grandmother Isis, Titi. Like her mother, Zeinab Hanem Anis, Titi is proud with a feather on her head. My father does not like that about her one bit. It irritates him that she's inherited the title *Hanem* long after those Ottoman titles were dropped, that she flaunts land and lineage long after she lost both, markers he's given up a long time ago. Titi doesn't like Baba either. She dislikes his rough mannerisms and blames it all on the lost land and family history.

He simply isn't like us, she says.

For years Baba is not welcome in Titi's home for Saturday lunches with the rest of the family. All due to the time she opened the door for him and watched him walk past her as if she were invisible.

Shouldn't you say hello to me when you walk into my house, Nizar? I might not be alive tomorrow.

I hope so, he says, muddling the words into a fake cough.

But Titi heard him alright, and though he insisted for years that he never said what she said she heard, he was once again a renegade.

In that interim, my mother, Nermin, and I leave him back in the apartment feeling all sorry for himself. I leave him with a twinge of guilt that eventually dissipates as the day turns into laughter around the dining table and endless up-to-no-good play with my cousins. From the window of Titi's bedroom, we would spy on the neighbors rolling between the bedsheets, their feet and shins—the only body parts visible to us—intertwining. We would run up and down the building, ringing doorbells and hiding, breaking into hysterical laughter when the neighbors opened their doors and found no one. At tea time, the family would gather again in the living room where more often than not Titi would criticize Baba openly. That was, until one day I could take it no more. I stand up. I shout at the whole room:

Stop it. He's my father for God's sake!

Cairo, 1987

I am living with Titi now, my mother, Nermin, and I, and my father is puff, gone. He moves so much that I lose track of his whereabouts. All I know is he must be wandering through new grounds, seeking edges, chasing the buck, his only currency for survival. He might be in Saudi Arabia or in Germany.

Being a child in Titi's household is tough. She likes all her things in order and impeccably clean. Most of her time is spent shouting at her help for being helpless, for not being as orderly as her, or as clean as her. She's up ladders in her satin shift polishing her floor-to-ceiling glass windows to a glistening crystal-clear, out on her balconies in a silk robe before noon tending her precious plants, or in the dining room polishing silverware. She relegates other home chores to me, the worst ones. I spend hours angry at the knotty fringe tassels on her Persian rugs I've been tasked with untangling. When I get tired, I make sure no one can see me before I grab the scissors and cut the knots off.

Titi shouts a lot at me, but that's no wonder. I do the exact opposite of everything she asks me to do. She tells me not to open the glass box with a geisha inside, the one grandpa Mohey bought her as a gift from Japan, but that's exactly what I do. I wait for her to get busy with one thing or another and I open that glass box. I snag the sequins or the embroidered threads on the geisha's kimono, one by one. It's hard for Titi to make me do what I don't want to do. Every morning I wake up before anyone, at 5:45 a.m., put a sausage pillow in my place in bed and hide. At 6 a.m., Titi comes to my bedroom to wake me up for school and doesn't find me. I watch her from my hiding place go from sleep mode to full panic mode. I only emerge when my school bus has come and gone, right at the point when she loses her mind. Titi shouts at me a lot, but that's no wonder. She's too old to be mothering. My father is gone and my mother works twelve-hour days. Nermin is easy to handle. She's quiet, avoidant, always with a book, and does what she's told whether she likes it or not; but me, I am trouble.

My mother goes to Paris for a week. She takes a much-needed break with a friend, something she has never done. My mother has never left us.

I cannot accept that she is leaving. I'm so filled with dread at the idea of being left to Titi that my insides are floating like flotsam in the dark waters. One parent leaving is hard, but two, and I'm on my knees. I'm on my knees begging her as she carries her suitcase and walks out the door.

Cairo, 1993

We're at Titi's house and so is Baba. He prefers to keep his distance even though he's been allowed back into the fold. We're all on a couch and he's in an armchair by the window, leaning tensely toward the TV. It's evening and the clouds outside are long shreds in white. He punctures an orange with both thumbs, then his face turns to stone.

On the screen, there's a white house, a lawn, and a white man sitting on a long brown wooden table, signing something. Behind him is a lineup of more white men and one brown one in a kuffiyyeh and a khaki suit. I make a noise and my mother shushes me with a dead stare and a finger to her lips. On the screen, the seated white man puts his pen down and gets up to take his place in the lineup behind him. The attendees stand up and clap. Everyone is shaking hands. The brown man in a kuffiyyeh has the biggest grin, the most eager handshake.

Baba gets up.

Kiss ikhtak bi ijri akhu sharmoota!

My mother covers my ears.

Please don't use this language in front of the children, she says.

Kiss ikhtak ya Arafat, he threw us under the bus, he threw all the Arabs of '48 under the bus.

The next day, on the morning bus ride to school, I ask an older kid about what Arafat did last night to warrant such a reaction. He tells me that for people like me and my father, it means we no longer have the right to return to Palestine.

Cairo, 1994

Nermin is twenty-three years old when she is put on suicide watch. Ever since Baba said he found her under a tree, things have been difficult. His words taught her things about this world, that it is a barren place where children lose their family trees. She had come to understand love as a spring that once was and has now dried up. Later when she fell in love, she could not unlearn it all.

His name was Hani, and before she met him, she'd only known dopamine from sugar. In a bitter world, sugar was the only reward. She mixed it with butter, slathered it on bread, sucked it off her fingers, and left its wrappers under her bed. Nermin loved sugar viciously, the way people love, because she was taught there is no gentle way to love. At first, her body knew how to break it, but then it didn't, so it stored it whole in her body for the cold winter nights, and there were many. The night when Baba found out she had a boyfriend and yanked her away from her date-night. The night when she cried in her pillow over a girl in school who had written *Fatso* under her photo in the yearbook in black bubble letters. The more she broke, the more she chased the dopamine, the more she consumed sugar, the more her body couldn't break it. It went on and on until life itself became an obtuse monster.

Nermin and Hani wrote for the same newspaper. He was in charge of the layout and she wrote the food column. He moved to Cairo from Alexandria and carried home with him, a peaceful place by the sea. He carried the Sidi Gaber train station, the morning fishing across the road from the train station, the salt of the Mediterranean from his balconies. Nermin fell in love with it all. The way he breezed into the office in the morning, the way he still managed to breeze through the office on a late night. For a second there, he was all the dopamine she needed, and they got engaged.

But Nermin could not unlearn it all, the barren tree, the dried-up spring. The years behind her cast a dark shadow over Hani's sea, and he ebbed.

The week after Hani broke the engagement, Mama took Nermin to a therapist. You need to watch her twenty-four seven, the therapist said, she might try to kill herself, before prescribing the anti-depressants.

Mama couldn't foot the bill, so she called +86, she called China, Baba:

We need your help, she said.

Call al-Adani, he said, inconvenienced, he'll give you money.

Al-Adani owned the shipping company Baba did business with in Egypt. In theory, he was the one who supplied our home's monthly allowance and university tuition from a running account he had with Baba, but in reality he was just Baba's buffer. More often than not he was instructed not to give Mama anything, neither money nor information.

Mama often drove me to al-Adani Shipping Company on Kasr El Nil Street and told me to go up on my own, delegate the humiliation. I'd sit and wait while he finished meetings and answered calls. He was not an uncle or family friend, so I just got right into what I needed when he was done with being busy.

Did Baba send us the money?

No, he'd say.

That night, after coming back from al-Adani's, I vowed to do everything in my power to bring Nermin back. I told stories, cracked jokes, brought out the board games and cards, and made her pancakes with honey. That night and for nights to come, I did not sleep. We lay on two single beds, and I held my breath while I watched her breathe. For a moment, my undivided attention was all the dopamine Nermin needed, and she came back. She came back, Hani came back, and they started to plan their wedding.

But Nermin's wedding required a venue, a wedding gown, a buffet, flowers, and again, Mama could not shoulder the costs alone, so she called +86, she called Baba:

Call al-Adani, he said.

I told Mama I wouldn't go up this time. Reluctantly, she called him herself.

My daughter, Nermin, she's getting married. Nizar told me he would be sending money for us.

Sorry, Nizar did not give me instructions.

Baba did not attend the wedding, either. He was busy, he said, he had business to attend to. Mama managed to throw a wedding for Nermin anyway. On a beautiful day with the sun shining bright, Nermin sparkled in white lace while Hani waited at the end of a leafy passageway decked with Arabian Jasmin. His bride walked toward him on the hand of our maternal uncle, Khalo Sherif.

After the first dance, the bride and groom sat at the head table, and a queue formed to congratulate them. I stood in line. When it was my turn to hug her and kiss her, I burst into tears.

What's wrong, Mai?

I am so sorry, I tried to say.

What?

I, I am sorry we fought so much.

Acre, 1935

Baba, do you remember how your mother used to take you to Tarshiha on weekend visits? It was a fifteen-minute drive from al-Kabri, where the almond trees grew by the hills. At dusk, Tarshiha's women would burn the logs for an outdoor fire pit and watch the flames crackle and pop. They would sing songs and roast almonds for the children. Your siblings would play a game called Blind Bear. They would include you, even though you were only three, on the condition that you be the blind bear. They would blindfold you, spin you around, and run. You would chase them, saying, I am the blind bear, I cannot see, but I carry a sword with me.

Your mother, Ibtihaj al-Qadi, came from Tarshiha. She was the daughter of Kamal al-Qadi, a wealthy landowner in his own right with land all the way to al-Kabri, just like Faris Serhan owned land all the way to Tarshiha.

There was so much wealth to go around, Baba, haven't you heard? Haven't you heard the story of Umm Mahmoud Fanous al-Safadi? She was picking apples from a tree one day by Abu Zidan al-Salw's home when she came across a boulder. She tried to push it, but it was too heavy, so she called Abu Zidan to help. When they finally managed to roll it over, they discovered a big hole, and in that hole, buried treasures of gold, silver, and Phoenician pottery. Didn't you know, our boon grew on trees and under the land's skin? Come dusk, come gust, come apples or gold?

On the day of the marriage proposal, Faris sent a delegation to Kamal al-Qadi's home in Tarshiha, as per custom, to ask for Ibtihaj's hand in marriage. We want your daughter Ibtihaj al-Qadi for our groom, Faris Serhan, they said, "with a dowry worth her weight in gold," and in response, Kamal al-Qadi said, blessings be to God the all-generous. Then the coffee and desserts were served and the ululations rang through the hills, through the orchards, to the sea.

Three months later, Faris and Ibtihaj invited their family and friends on a trip to Acre. They went to buy the bride's jewelry and trousseau and capped the day with lunch in a restaurant by the sea. At sunset, they returned to al-Kabri as the light turned the color of peach and the roads flickered with beeswax candles. Everyone turned out to greet them by the village entrance, tossing rice in their path for rain and prosperity.

They danced dabkeh and stomped their feet for love, for hope, for joy. They chanted in praise of the Prophet Muhammad and recited poems. Out in the fields, the women gathered the olive branches for the fire. In the kitchen they boiled the buttermilk to soak the pastry. On her henna night, Ibtihaj had her hands etched and received gifts of soap and perfume. On the wedding night, she slipped on the white dress. It took a whole village to embroider that dress. All the while they sang:

Wheat-skin, small waist
moon-like face with a beauty spot
bows and arrows on either side
eyes like deer and the night
the color of kohl in your eyes.

Cairo, 1989

I am just like any other child. I think my parents are big just because I am small. They tell me what to do, so they must be in control. They have come this far, so they know how to survive. I'm just like any other child in the back seat, I don't know that the drivers are children too, all grown up and stunted in their growth. It's all bumper cars and people switching lanes, suddenly. It doesn't occur to me that my mother and father have no idea where they're going. I trust them. I trust that however bumpy the road is, it is not their fault, and it is the only way to go.

But sometimes things calm down. My father would turn into a child who plays nice. Back in the apartment on Orabi Street, he would sit still and let me play with him the way I played with my dolls: paint his face with blue eye-shadow and red lipstick, tie the few wisps of hair on his head in a little bow, and clip Mama's earrings to his ears. When the mood was right, he would race me back and forth from the living room to the fridge right outside the kitchen. We would reach the finish line at the same time and bang our hands on the cool stainless-steel door as hard as we could. My mum would run out of the kitchen and say, I have three children not two. These are the moments where I float, suspended in disbelief. I tell myself, this is home.

Cairo, 1990

My mother packs a bag to leave. She opens the door and I grab at her skirt. She leaves anyway. In the living room where Baba weeps, I turn the TV on and the volume up. At sunset, I get up to turn the lights on.

No, he says.

Darkness falls over both of us and all I see is shadows, all I hear is his ghosts and their moans.

Two weeks later, my mother comes back. She puts her bag down and pulls half her hair up, and I see. I see what's underneath, big bald patches of pink skin with dots where hair follicles are supposed to be. The patches are like continents on a map I do not recognize, and I'm lost.

It's alopecia areata, she tells me.

What is that?

It's from depression, your hair falls.

Will it grow back?

They have to inject steroids into my scalp.

How many times?

Grief and loss show up in one's body to warn, to scream that this is no way to live. For the next three months, my mother pleads for a divorce as her hair sprouts back, but my father can't bear to lose her. It's his prerogative to grant a divorce anyway, so he doesn't.

Cairo, 1991

Anis Salama is a success story. He has come a long way since that time in his brother Mohsen's office where he challenged him to a duel. Dashingly handsome, charismatic, and Swiss-made, having been the first Egyptian with a degree from *Ecole Hôtelière de Lausanne*, followed by a glitzy career in the hotel business, he is now the President of the Egyptian Hotel Association and the paterfamilias of Mama's family. He has every reason to be proud, with a feather on his head just like his sister, Isis, and just like his mother, Zeinab Hanem Anis.

My mother, desperate for a divorce, pleads with her uncle Anis to intervene. Anis Salama calls my father and summons him to his office. He is busy and pissed and skips the niceties.

You will divorce Nana today. You don't want trouble now, do you?

The very next day, my parents sign their divorce papers. I come back from school and my mother approaches me with caution. She suspects her breaking news will break me.

Your dad and I signed the divorce papers today, she says.

Hallelujah.

You're not upset?

I am upset.

Oh darling, come here.

No, I say, I'm upset you didn't divorce earlier.

I stayed for you and your sister.

You shouldn't have.

I don't remember him packing his bags or saying good-bye. I do not see him leave. I do not remember his new Cairo address or how long he stayed before finally leaving. All I remember is that sometimes I'd spot him in one café or another around Cairo, a lone wolf, people-watching; his loneliness so unbearable that I would turn my gaze down, pretend not to see him, and keep walking.

Following her divorce, Mama starts to refer to herself as a cat and to Nermin and me as her kittens. We're no kittens and she by no means means to be cute. What Mama means is, there's a storm outside and she must carry us to safety the way cats hold their litter by the scruff and scram across a highway.

Mama, I know you're listening. I'm older now. I am wild-eared and on my own. This world has many roads, yet none of them lead to home. This world is treacherous and all the wheels keep skidding. Everywhere I look, I see tails and horns. By your love, don't leave me.

Yiwu, 2000

Ou pretends I am not there. Every morning she walks over from Baba's apartment building to our hotel and joins us at the breakfast table.

Good morning, she greets him, taking her place by his side.

Good morning, Ou, I say.

I'm suddenly struck by a feeling— I miss Hongxi. There's a Lebanese client in town, Baba tells Ou, he owns a toy store chain in Beirut. Ou must take him, and me, to the Yiwu Toy Market.

We meet the client in the hotel reception. His name is Khaled. I check him out. He is young, 30s tops. He is warm and relaxed as he shakes my hand, and for the first time in a long while, I don't feel like a spectacle to be stared at or awkwardly overlooked. We get to talking and walking and his easiness rubs off on me, bringing a spring to my step. Ou follows, for once, and soon recedes to the background, and I pretend she is not there.

At the entrance to the Yiwu Toy Market, I look up and see five floors over-stacked with merchandise. The sheer superabundance makes my jaw drop. This is where the world's worth of toys is made, where the ubiquitous Made in China label originates. Every country, city, town and remote village carries these products. Every depart-ment store, shabby shop, stall, and hole-in-the-wall. For a moment, I feel like I'm smack in the epicenter of the world. I'm giddy and it's infectious, and soon Khaled gets giddy too.

Khaled and I forget business and run up and down the market like children. We play with toys that spin, fly, run on tracks, light up in neon color, and glow in the dark. We lie down on plush stuffed animals ten times our size. We bounce rubber chicken on rope and fool around with talking robots. We wear party wigs and blow rocket balloons. I stop at Barbie: her glam pool, her ultimate closet, her dream dollhouse. I did not know this all-American dream is made in China too. I marvel at the details of her perfect life, BBQ grille on the lawn, and elevator to access all three floors of her mansion, a ten-bedroom with a glittery closet, balconies, a pet play area, and a carport for her pink van.

Have you ever had the dream house? Khaled asks. He offers me a cigarette. I light it up.

Never.

Let's get you one.

What would I do with it now?

It doesn't matter.

I turn to look at Ou and my smile freezes. Her face has turned to stone, but her eyes, her dark eyes are welling up with tears. She despises me, and for the life of me, I don't know why. Whatever narrative she's built up in her head, I am not privy to, and yet it seems I am the villain.

That night, Baba tells me I should step aside. He and Ou will be taking care of Khaled's business for the rest of his trip.

The next day, I venture out for lunch on my own. I find a restaurant and check the menu before I sit down.

There's tomato soup, so I order a bowl. While I wait for it to arrive, I begin to notice that some of the people sitting down to eat have stopped their conversations to look at me. I'm so tired of it, I begin a staring match with a group of young women on my right. I stare until they find it funny and laugh. They whisper in each other's hair and point their fingers at me. Soon, the whole restaurant gets a rise out of our interaction and begins to whisper too. It multiplies and multiplies until my tomato soup arrives. I stare inside my bowl looking for any signs of tomato, but all I see is transparent soup with a boiled egg and angel hair. I signal to the waiter.

I ordered a tomato soup.
抱歉。我不明白。
But this is not a tomato soup.
你不要嗎?
The women laugh out loud, and soon enough their laughter catches on. Every table, everyone.

Pack this for me, I tell the waiter, takeaway please.
But I cannot wait for my takeaway bag. Fuck it, it's not even tomato soup. I leave some money on the table, put my jacket on and get the hell out.

It's 3 p.m. and I don't want to go back to the hotel. There are no English-speaking channels on TV and the only place with internet is the business center on the ground floor. With time to kill before Baba returns, I decide to revisit the Yiwu Toy Market.

At the gate, an old woman walks out, taking slow baby steps forward. She is back-bent, oblivious to the comings and goings around her, to the world that is changing, to the fact that Arabs like me have started to trickle in. She looks up and sees me, except that she doesn't really see me. She sees someone or something, an anagram of a human. She sees the devil in me, it seems, and starts to scream. I jolt back. She's old, I think, I ought to give her a pass, I should calm her down, assure her that although I'm not Chinese, I'm still human. I come closer to her, reach for her hand.

I'm sorry, I tell her.

But the woman does not want me near her. She falters backwards, falls to the ground, and begins to scream for help. Crowds form. Some watch, bemused; others help the woman, now in tears. I run. The faster I run, the harder I cry.

I cry all the way to the hotel and until night falls in the hotel room. I cry until my head explodes, because I know. I know the time has come. It's time to leave, to leave him. It's been six months, thousands of miles away, led by a chronic and compulsive escapist, following in the footsteps of a decomposing foot.

At night, Baba walks in, spent, and finds my face swollen, tissues scattered around me on the bed.

What's wrong? he asks.

Baba calls Hongxi in Shenzhen and tells him to come to Yiwi. He is to accompany me on the long ride out. A couple of days later, we are at the Yiwu Trade City Bus Station. Our bus door is open; the engine is heaving. I stand in front of Baba with my suitcases. My baggage overwhelms me. My mind is caught in a whirring loop: I can't stay; I can't leave him. Over and over again.

Goodbye, is all Baba says.

He holds my shoulders, as if any more words would result in the most ridiculous thing. I drop my head onto his chest, feel his heat, his hurry, his faint heartbeat, and do the most ridiculous thing.

You're crying?

Come with me, Baba.

With you, where?

Home. I mean, wherever you want.

I want to be here.

Please.

Get on the bus, *habibti*.

I shake my head and sob until my legs give way. He cups my face, he kisses my forehead.

Sweetheart, come on. Get on the bus.

The distance between Yiwu and Shenzhen is 963 kilometers, that is twelve hours by bus. It would've taken six hours if I had taken a plane and eight hours if I had taken a train, but Baba only knows tough love. I wonder if Hongxi had come here by bus. If he did, I wouldn't know. He shows no signs of strain, of fatigue; quiet resolve is all he gives off. For a long time, all I see is green mountains sweeping backwards, the cliffy Songpu Hills, the flying gulls over Xiuhu Lake, perhaps a few pagodas, perhaps some red temples with gold-glazed roofs and manicured gardens. I can no longer tell. The roads I leave behind are as impeccable as computer graphics with not a blemish in sight, and yet my tears water down the imagery. Or is it raining outside? I can no longer tell.

I am sorry, Miss Mai, Hongxi says in Arabic.

It's okay, Hongxi.

We get off the bus at night in Guangdong and transfer to a second bus at Dongguan Nancheng. For the next two hours, all views fade to black. The gentle rocking of the bus lulls me to sleep, and I dream.

I dream of Ou. It's the dead of the night and she's sitting at the foot of Titi's bed in Cairo, stationary, while Titi sleeps. The cupboards are open and emptied. Titi's clothes are piled up on the floor. In their place are a few tiny dresses on hangers.

Ou, I whisper, what are you doing here?

She gets up, her back straight as a sword, and stares at me through eyes that look like two black wells. I notice the ladder stitches running up her long legs. She walks to the vintage Singer sewing machine, the one Titi used to sew Mama's tiny dresses a long time ago. She sits down in front of it.

Don't turn it on, I say, you'll wake up Titi.

She starts the machine. The needle whirrs over tiny gloves.

Beirut, 1993

It's not the first time I leave my father. The first time was the summer after my school graduation, a summer spent arguing over what university I should apply for. Or rather, what university they were going to send me to. My father claimed that the private American University in Cairo, with its dollar tuition for foreigners, was too expensive, and that I would be attending Cairo University instead. My mother put her foot down.

No. Mai will go to AUC.

But my father wasn't about to grant my mother her wish, even if it was my wish too, even though he had the money. He needed to get back at her at any cost, even if that cost was me.

That summer, I joined him in Beirut where he announced an alternative plan. I was to study Graphic Design at the Lebanese American University.

But Baba, I have no interest in graphic design.

The move was to try to reclaim me as his own, and he had it all worked out. I would live with Teta in the apartment in Corniche al-Mazra'a, and, through the Hariri Foundation, secure a scholarship to a university in Lebanon.

Leading me by the hand from one application to the next, Baba spoke with much admiration about the son of a grocer who had become a billionaire prime minister. How in 1982, Rafic al-Hariri had donated twelve million dollars to Lebanese victims of the 1978 South Lebanon conflict, how he put the country back on the map and helped clean up a demolished Beirut with his own money, slowly but surely turning the city once again into the Paris of the Middle East, with dainty, pastel-colored buildings and designer stores. Just like Baba, Rafic al-Hariri was a college drop-out whose luck had turned suddenly, and in a big way. Baba saw himself in him, and I felt totally stuck. I did not want to leave Cairo, or my mother, or my friends. I didn't want to live with Teta in Beirut.

No one owned a mobile phone at the time, and I didn't want to call my mother from the Serhan family home. The next day, I told Baba I was going for a walk and, from a phone booth, called +2 02. I called my mother in Cairo.

Mama, help. Baba wants to keep me here.

She called him. She called my uncles, and she called Teta.

Help, she said, he is keeping my daughter against her will.

That summer, my father's siblings pressured him to concede. They argued that he should keep me out of his issues with my mother. I returned to Egypt and enrolled in the American University in Cairo.

Acre, pre-1948

Baba, in Acre the mountains, sea, and breeze co-existed. The water, fifty meters below land, flowed freely from coast to spring, all the way down under the land's skin. People, together under crescents, crosses, and stars, moved freely too, from Judaea to Jerusalem to Jericho. It didn't matter at all, once.

There was a simpler time, when all the residents of Palestine were known as Palestinian. The Jewish people, once a small community of faith based in the highlands and foothills of Judea, were called Abna' Falastin, Children of Palestine. They were not a race, there was no racism, until the white man made it so. He rounded them up from Morocco, Iraq, Yemen, Ethiopia, Russia, Hungary, and Poland. He homogenized a myriad and one cultures. He theologized, theorized, victimized, erased, and narrativized, and called it history.

Do you remember Naharia, that Jewish settlement in Acre long before settlements took on a whole new meaning? It was twelve minutes away from al-Kabri on the Mediterranean Sea. The Jews there were Sephardic. They spoke Arabic and were part of the fabric of your neighborhood. Your family used to take you to Naharia on Friday mornings for coffee and desserts in an outdoor café by the sea. As you relished a pastry, sea fret on your face, you heard Abu Daoud, the Jewish butcher, son of Palestine, say into the microphone, Glory be to God who made this halal meat for all of us. Allahu Akbar! Everyone heard him three villages away. He would then raise his cleaver over the cow's head and, with a swift incision to the throat, cut the windpipes. On your way back to al-Kabri, Teta would stop at Abu Daoud's to buy her meat.

Naharia also had the best dentists and eye doctors in Acre, long before Lebanese doctors moved to Palestine and excelled in those fields. Teta used to go to a German dentist, a Sephardic Jew, for her teeth. One day the dentist had a problem, and she thought, who better than Faris Serhan to call for help?

Faris Effendi, she said, only you can help me. Someone stole my cow!

Faris Serhan made one phone call and, by the end of the day, had the thief arrested and the cow returned to its owner. The dentist was so grateful that when she went home to Germany on vacation, she bought your parents a tea set as a thank you gift. The tea set was so dainty that Teta fled Palestine with it in 1948.

Beirut, 1975

The tea set moved from al-Kabri to Ras Beirut and from Ras Beirut to Corniche al-Mazra'a. When the Lebanese Civil War broke in Lebanon, Teta had to flee again, this time to Cyprus, leaving the tea set behind. She moved to Limassol and spent fourteen years waiting for the war to end. In that interim, squatters took over her apartment in Beirut. Fourteen years later, the war ended and Teta needed to return to her apartment, but the squatters would not leave without a lawsuit, without a legal eviction notice, without throwing the tea set from the balcony and smashing it into fine porcelain powder.

Beirut, 2001

It's been six months since I left China. In those six months, I apply for a job in Cairo as a copywriter in an advertising agency. I do not know how else to use my degree in English Literature to make a living. I have no portfolio of work yet, so I hand some of my university essays to the boss interviewing me. My would-be boss takes a look at the writing and says,

> This needs to be simpler. Write as if you're addressing a fifth-grader.

I do that. I dumb the writing down and throw myself into the rat race, until one day I receive a call from Baba. He's relented, finally. His foot is causing him so much pain. He tells me he needs me to fly to Beirut for a doctor consultation.

I take time off work. I fly in from Cairo and he flies in from China and, upon arrival, we book a doctor's appointment for the next day. In Teta's living room, the *manakeesh*, *knafeh*, and coffee are served per usual upon our arrival. I watch him make some calls. I notice that he is wearing loafers on his left foot and a slipper on his right. I notice that the right foot looks like a third-degree burn.

> Get up, he says to me, hanging up the phone.

> What, I say, licking *za'tar* off my fingers, where are you going?

He leans half his weight on my shoulder and staggers forward.
We're going to meet Malik in Ayn al-Mreiseh.
Malik who?

Ayn al-Mreiseh shares the same Mediterranean waters as Alexandria, with ice-cream parlors, coffee houses, and a huge Ferris wheel that the eye can see from one end of the sea promenade to the other. The skyline, however, looks strikingly different than in Alexandria. Thanks to Prime Minister Rafic al-Hariri's strong ties with the Saudi royal family, enough money has been pumped into construction to restore the Manara skyline to its original glitz. Multimillion-dollar skyscrapers and hotels with panoramic sea views now stand high over sweeping blue waters, with tower cranes and dump trucks everywhere in sight.

We settle in a café and Malik arrives. He's handsome, I take note, uncomfortably so. Tall, to begin with. His hair is a perfect chestnut color with tips that turn copper in the sun. Some copper in his stubble too. Malik has bags under his eyes, though, like a lot of sleepless nights, but the eyes themselves are brightly lit in brown. He's got small, fine features. *Misamsim* is how one would describe him in Egyptian, as in, as fine as sesame.

He reaches our table and does what all my father's business associates do. He hugs him and gives me a hastened nod. He sits close to him, as far from me as awkwardly possible. He addresses him only and keeps his eyes down when I speak.

They talk business and more business, and I discover that Malik is married with children, that business in Beirut is dire. He is struggling financially and hangs all his future hopes on my father. He is now the protégé who is moving to China to learn the ropes.

I sit quietly, invisibly, and wonder why I'm here. By now I have a job in Cairo. By now my father should have lost all hope that I would return to China. Assumptions bounce back and forth in my head.

I am here so that I will know who my replacement is in China, to regret it. I am here because Baba is hoping that someday, Malik and I will take over, together. I am here because he is showing me off. He is proud of me, perhaps, because I'm all grown up. I look like my mama, Nana, that girl from Cairo whom he fell in love with. Or I am here because he is relishing this control he exerts over Malik by showing me to him and daring him to come close. Malik is there to be intimidated, it seems, to be shown his place and its limits in a new power dynamic, and for his loyalties to be tested.

Acre, pre-1948

Exile led you to believe everywhere was a threat and everyone was in your way. I do not blame you, Baba, but I wish you'd understood, it was no way to live. It could've saved us, it might've even saved you.

Let me take you back to the origin story: The small community of Sephardic Jews in Palestine were different than the Ashkenazim who arrived on streamliners—thirty-five thousand following the Balfour Declaration, another seventy thousand fleeing Nazi gas chambers, and many more thousands in between. The Sephardic Jews were friendly to our people. They traded with them and spoke their language. The Ashkenazim, however, did not. They refused to learn Arabic and, as a matter of principle, boycotted our shops and labor. They stood guard at the orchards they had bought to prevent the Palestinian farmers from getting jobs there. Following the closing of the Agricultural Bank, they prevented farmers from obtaining credit, leaving them to sell part of their land in order to develop the rest or to turn to moneylenders who charged some thirty percent interest. They swam naked in our springs, shocking the village people. They poured kerosene on our tomatoes, smashed our eggs, and attacked our cars.

Do you remember that one time when your family drove along the Acre coast and encountered a truck full of Ashkenazim? They stuck their tongues out. Wait for it, they signaled. You were in their way, so they threatened you. They were in your way, too.

Beirut, 2001

Cars, cars are air-locked with my father seated by my side. The taxi driver is driving us to Jbeil for the doctor's appointment, and no amount of fresh mountain breeze or cedar trees can diffuse the smell of deep decay, of roots lost, of roads traversed, of air still with reckoning. We drive up through winding mountains, the clock tock-ticking backwards.

The doctor's home is a log cabin hidden in the mountains. Inside is dim-lit, with rugs made of cowhide and wildlife mounted on the walls. I stare at a decapitated deer head on the wall while the doctor tells Baba to raise his foot up on an ottoman. In the deer's dark and glassy eyes, I see Baba's reflection, I see his right foot and deaths within deaths.

How could you wait this long? the doctor asks.
I turn to look. The doctor bends over the foot and with his index finger cuts a slice of air to demonstrate:

> We are going to have to amputate, he says gesturing toward the toes and down the ball of the foot. From here all the way down to here.

The amputation is a quick procedure, twenty to sixty minutes tops. The doctors make an incision into the skin of the foot. They cut off the muscle. Tie off and seal the blood vessels to stop the bleeding. Cut through the bone. They remove the dead part and pull the muscles over the bone. They pull the skin over the muscles. They sew to form a stump, then dress the foot in gauze, to let it breathe.

For aftercare, Baba takes medication for pain relief and the prevention of blood clots. He has to raise his leg to ease the swelling. I have to apply ice packs and give him baths. He must rest. He must delay his return to work.

Cairo, 1985

I come back from school to our apartment on Wadi El Nil Street to find Baba alone in the living room. The air is still, but there's a tremor in the walls. The sound coming out of him is malformed, like a tone-deaf whimper.

I go searching for Mama, find her in bed staring at the ceiling. I ask her, what is going on? She tells me my grandfather, Faris Serhan, passed away today in Beirut.

I go back to Baba and sit next to him, but he's completely turned inwards, toward a womb or a war. I try to move his hands away from his face, to hold him, to tell him to come back, *look at me*. When he does, I see that his nose is bleeding.

And I did not know then what I know now. That day, Baba cried for much more than a father. He cried for the place where we're from.

Beirut, 1985

The next day, my father flies to Beirut from Cairo, Amo Jamal flies in from Amman, Amo Nabil flies in from Jeddah, Amto Nadia flies in from Qatar, and Amto Aida flies in from Oman. Amo Nasser could not make it all the way from America.

Teta holds it together in the funeral, keeps all the pieces in one place. She takes condolences sitting down, makes small conversation. The Arab Higher Committee office in Beirut takes charge of a formal funeral procession to the Sabra and Shatila Cemetery, where Faris Serhan is laid to rest.

Acre, 1948

Baba, I know you don't want to look back at tapered leaves or torched homes, but it is all in you, there is nowhere to hide. Time is about to stop, so stop running, hear me out:

On March 14, 1948, Fadl Balquis sold his wife's jewelry, his cattle, and his land to donate money to the Arab Salvation Army in exchange for arms secured from the Arab Military Committee in Damascus.

On March 21, with some hand grenades in his pocket, Fadl walked to the ancient mill. He went to meet other freedom fighters, Mustafa Balquis, Omar al-Ashouh, Mohamed al-Masri, Tawfiq Yacoub, Omar al-Jishi, Abu Hussein Qaddura, Hajj Abu Nimr Hamad, Abu Moussa Balquis, Muhammed al-Dabbagh, and Salih al-Jishi. They all got on a bus heading to al-Birwa, 10.5 kilometers east of Acre.

On the way, Salih al-Jishi had half his body out of the bus window when a grenade went off by accident in his pocket. Salih looked at his ripped pants and found blood. He imagined the worst. He searched wildly between his thighs and found his manhood intact. The damage was to his leg. Salih al-Jishi jumped for joy on one foot. The men on the bus did not know what to do with him, so they drove back to al-Kabri, dropped him off, and headed to al-Birweh.

Around noon, word reached them that the Haganah had spread in a neighboring village and were heading to al-Kabri next through Naharia. The men decided to stop and block the road with whatever they could find.

They were piling up rocks and stones when they saw an armored vehicle drive toward them. It stopped at the roadblock. The men inside it were dressed in Orlite helmets and olive green shirts. They spoke in foreign tongue, in Hebrew. The driver reversed, shouting something about the authority vested in him by the King of England, before charging forward and bulldozing his way over the rocks.

Three armored vehicles, two lorries, and a bus followed with more Orlite helmets. The men of al-Kabri fired at one armored vehicle loaded with ammunition until it burst into flames. The armored convoy halted in its tracks and members of the Jewish militia stepped out.

All hell broke loose.

The Haganah spread amongst the orchards and opened fire. Al-Kabri's men fought back with old Sten guns, English rifles, and hand grenades. The blood bath lasted until dawn, until every Orlite helmet was on the ground. Fadl Balquis and his men seized eleven rifles and seven boxes of ammunition that morning, before sleeping under the trees.

At the time, Teta Ibtihaj was in Tarshiha visiting her mother. She had taken you and all your brothers and sisters with her with the exception of your eldest brother,

Jamal, who had accompanied your father and the Grand Mufti of Jerusalem, Hajj Amin al-Husseini, to a conference in Lebanon.

Back home in al-Kabri, Teta had let all the help go for the night. In the morning, her helper, Hajjeh Fatimeh, was in her own home sifting through pebbles in rice when she heard what sounded like an air strike hit nearby land. She ran out of her home and through the olive groves toward the plumes of smoke. She ran toward the spring of Ayn Kabri where she saw what she never un-saw: a ball of fire the size of a boulder crashing into the water and the spring blowing up into a million droplets. She saw bobwhites chased by shrapnel, their wings catching fire.

Hajjeh Fatimeh ran and ran until she got to the home of your father, Faris Serhan.

Beirut, 2001

Baba leaves the hospital after a successful amputation and returns to the apartment in Corniche al-Mazra'a. Two days later, it's time for a bath.

I sit him on a stool in the bathtub and turn to face the wall while he takes off his clothes. I have never seen him naked.

I need your help getting my pants off, he says.

I turn and see no details, only lasting impressions: Body beaten, skin in tatters, fossil, father. I straighten his leg, prop his bandaged foot on the bathtub ledge. I hold on to his trouser cuffs and gently slip them over his bandaged foot. The rot is now sanitized with sprays and ointments, but the stench of decaying skin is still lodged in my chest. I reach out for the sponge and the soap, lather one with the other, and squeeze the sponge over his body.

We lie on two single beds that evening. By nightfall he's restless. He's not built to stay in one place.

Come on, he says, let's go.

Go where?

Let's go for a walk in the Solidaire.

No. No way, I'm not going.

He sits up, pulls himself along until he reaches the foot of the bed.

You are not going, I say.

101

He grabs a shirt, puts it on.
What are you doing?
I am going.
No, you're not.
Ssssh.
No.
Shush!

He drags his foot to Solidaire, and we stop in a hookah café where he orders a coffee and lights a cigarette. We sit quietly for a long time, looking in different directions.
What? he eventually says.
What?
Talk to me.
About what?
Something light.
Alright, I say, turning to face him, this is wrong. What you're doing is wrong. They told you to stay home. The doctor said that.
Ya Allah, shush!
No.
Ya Mai, ya habibty, I cannot retire and come live here.
Why?
I'm not done.
What more?
You want to know?
He stubs a cigarette in the ashtray and lights another one, draws a deep breath before moving closer to me.
I'm done being an agent, the middleman, he whispers in my ear, I want to be the source.

What do you mean, source?

I'm building my own factory.

For what?

Children's clothing.

I feel like shaking him, like pulling my hair out, but instead I turn my whole body away and pretend to people-watch.

Mai, order a taxi, he says, suddenly.

I turn to look at him. His head is unscrewed on his neck, his eyes are fading. I grab his chair before he falls off.

Baba, you okay?

Just order a taxi.

I make a phone call, place the taxi order, and try to give him a sip of my lemonade. He refuses. When the driver calls to say he's waiting on the street corner, I lift him off his chair and put his arm around my shoulder. He drags his right foot forward for a few meters then his body gives in. The world turns and he collapses to the ground, bringing me down with him. I get up. I do not know if he's dead or alive, so I start screaming.

Baba sits in the passenger seat of the taxi, eyes closed, and it's pouring rain outside.

> Listen, he says, don't you dare tell Teta or Amto or anyone back home what just happened. Understood?

Back home, he greets the family and slumps on the nearest chair. They begin to criticize him for going out. They tell him he should consider retiring. They question why he still wants to be in China. They argue that he's made enough to now rest and live a good life. My father can no longer walk, cannot escape from room to room, so he lowers his gaze and says nothing.

Everyone drifts back to Lebanese politics on TV.

I go out on the balcony and close the shutters, lock myself out. Outside, the rain is pouring and the cold grips my skin. The balcony tiles are wet, my coat will soon be soaked, but I don't care. I slide my back down the wall until my butt lands in the puddle, and I stay there.

Cairo, 1995

Back on Orabi Street, where we are all living when we are still we, the apartment is tiny. My friends come over and have no place to sit but in the bedroom I share with Nermin. I am in my early teens, and all my girlfriends and I want to do is to talk about boys, and it's all top secret, but Nermin doesn't get it. She's just happy to have people around, so she sticks around. I go out to the living room.

Mama, Nermin is in the room.

And?

My friends are here.

Where should she go?

I don't know. We want to talk freely. Do something. Mama tells Nermin to take her studies and go sit on the dining table, and all hell breaks loose. We start fighting. We fight like cats and dogs.

Back in the apartment on Orabi Street, there is one bathroom and four of us. I never walk in or out by my own free will. Someone has to bang on the bathroom door and pester me until I come out. There are too many of us in this space. Too much of each of us. For any other family, a tiny space might be okay. Each family has its own genes and every gene pool lives differently. Ours just happens to live with ghosts, and fields burning and fractious feet.

Acre, 1948

They disagreed over a fortress called Jideen two kilometers north of al-Kabri. The zionists claimed their historic right to it, and so did the Palestinians.

It was built in 1220 CE by the Teutonic Knights, a small, voluntary and mercenary army that had served as a crusading military order for the protection of Christians in the Holy Land. The fortress was destroyed by the Mamluk King al-Zahir Baybars, Sultan of Egypt and the Levant, between 1268 and 1271. Its ruins remained in place until Zahri al-Omar, ruler of Palestine under the Ottoman Empire, rebuilt it and gave it the name "Jideen Castle" in 1760, only for it to be destroyed once again by Ahmed Basha al-Jazzar, ruler of Sidon province in the Levant. It sat there in ruins for hundreds of years, gathering dust, sheep, and shrubs, with Bedouins for inhabitants.

Beirut, 2002

Four months have passed. Four months since Baba fainted in Beirut's Solidaire, since he limped his way back to China to open a new factory.

We meet again in Beirut. He picks me up from Rafic al-Hariri International Airport. He sits in the passenger seat next to the taxi driver and I sit in the back. Without turning to look at me he says,

> Your Amo Nabil passed away today in Jeddah. Brain tumor.

I'm not allowed to cry of course, so I bury my head between my legs and do it quietly. I remember Amo Nabil's trips to Cairo, how they all felt like Christmas. How he spared no expense on us, bought me my first Sony Walkman. How he took Nermin and me out for ice-cream or to the theater. How he hugged us when things were rough. How he spoke to Baba to try and fix things at home, to fix him. Amo Nabil was handsome and kind and generous and always impeccably dressed.

That night after the funeral, Baba calls me into the empty living room. He asks me to close the partition door and sit down. Then he speaks:

> Listen, Mai. I want you to know that if anything happens to me, you and your sister are financially secure for the rest of your lives.

I get up. Try to walk away from words and their heat, but he grabs me by the wrist.

Sit down.

I don't wanna hear it.

You have to. Sit, this is important. If anything happens to me, he repeats, there are two accounts in the Bank of China. One is in Chinese renminbi and the other is in US dollar. The passcode for the renminbi account is Nermin's birthday. The passcode for the US dollar account is your birthday. Remember this.

Cairo, 2002

It is 4 a.m. and all signs of life have been absorbed by the dark. I'm fast asleep when my mobile rings. It's a Chinese voice, a woman.

你好，諾拉.
Hello?
Yes, ni hao. Mai, Nizar, he 有 five 天.
I am sorry, who is this?
It is Ou.
I sit up.
Yes, Ou. What are you saying?
Nizar, 病得很重. He 有 five 天.
He has five what?
You come to China.
Where is he? Can I talk to him?
No, hospital. Come.

The next day I go to the Chinese Embassy. I tell the man behind the acrylic barrier that my father is in critical condition in hospital and I need an expedited visa, that I need to travel immediately. The man tells me, processing time is two weeks. He is matter of fact about it, won't budge. I go home. At home I dial + 86 1, I call China, my father.

Alo, Mai.

He's picked up, and his voice is strong, like none of what Ou said was true.

   Baba, what is going on?

   I am fine.

   What do you mean, you are fine? Ou is saying—

   I am telling you, I am fine. Don't believe anyone here. Listen, book me a flight to Beirut.

   I don't think you should get on a plane in this condition.

   Listen to me and do as you are told. I will not stay here. Book me the first flight to Cairo, tomorrow. You and Nermin will meet me at the airport. We will fly together to Beirut, and I will check into the American University Hospital. Send the e-ticket by email.

   I don't think—

He hangs up.

I book tickets for all: Tickets for Nermin and her newborn, Ali, and me, and a ticket for Baba, which I send to his Hotmail, nizarserhan@hotmail.com. The plan is for him to fly out of China and transfer from Bangkok to Dubai, and then Cairo, where we would accompany him to Beirut.

We reach Cairo International Airport and wait for him. Time passes and he does not show up. I go up to the airline counter and ask them to check the manifest to know whether he boarded the plane from Guangzhou or not. They check and come back to me.

The manifest shows that he boarded the plane from Guangzhou to Bangkok but did not board his next flight from Bangkok to Dubai.

We have no way of reaching him. Nermin and I decide to board the flight to Beirut anyway. Maybe when we're with the rest of the family, we will be able to think more clearly. Maybe we'll find him in Beirut.

We land in Rafic al-Hariri Airport and find Amo Jamal and Malik waiting for us in the arrival hall. They run toward us.

Where is your Dad? Where is Nizar?

We get to Teta's house in Corniche al-Mazra'a. The house is filled with worried and hurried bodies. Neighbors, cousins, even Amto Nadia is here from Qatar.

Where is your dad? Where is Nizar?

I don't know. I don't know.

Malik's on the phone, call after call, +966, +861, +66, +961. His face is tense and I wonder what worries him so much. My father will show up. It's only a matter of time before we find him.

Teta is in her room, supine and staring at the ceiling. Her Alzheimer's is a blessing right now. It shields her from what's happening. She might not even remember who Nizar is.

My brain shutters shut and I go into a room, shut myself in. I busy myself with the most beautiful creature I've ever seen, my new nephew, Ali. What a gorgeous child he is, his skin, its rolls, its biscuit smell. Nothing about him is yet touched by this world. Until I can take it no more and will myself to sleep.

In the middle of the night, I hear hard banging on the door. I put a pillow over my head. Whoever they are, whatever news they bring, I do not wish to hear it.

Acre, 1948

Baba,

Bear with me. We're almost there, the origin story. You must come with me. You must not forget to breathe.

It was May 21, 1948. The mail, which was normally distributed to the nearby towns and villages from Tarshiha, hadn't arrived that day. Your mother, now back in al-Kabri, heard that the truck carrying the mail had been attacked by zionist militia on the road. Word reached her that they were taking people prisoners in the nearby towns, that there were executions, that pregnant women were being stabbed in the stomach, that their zionist commander had ordered the following: "To attack with the aim of capturing the villages of al-Kabri, Umm al-Faraj, and al-Nahr, to kill the men and to destroy and set fire to the villages." Word reached her that this particular operation was in retaliation for the killing of eleven people in a zionist convoy two months earlier.

Then the phone rang. It was your father, Faris, from Beirut. He told your mother to leave immediately, to come to Beirut and wait there for the war to end.

Your mother didn't have time to pack. What packing when children were being killed, when bodies were burning, with guns blasting and glass shattering, while animals ran loose down the dirt tracks? Some villagers took the keys to their homes and forgot the doors wide open. Others forgot their wedding bands by their bedside tables or the coffee surging over a fire. Your mother took her children, two gallons of olive oil, and the tea set the Jewish doctor from Naharia had gifted her, then hopped on a truck heading to Beirut with her family. On the way, she spotted her village people running through the trees, into mosques and abandoned schools while she mumbled broken verses from the Quran.

Keep listening, Baba, and keep breathing. Breathe through the crossing of the Palestinian border, past Saida in the south of Lebanon, to Beirut.

When your mother left, dawn was choking in black smoke: The Haganah grabbed people by the hair and kicked them all the way to the center of town where they fell unconscious. A village lying flat under fire, under rubble, men, women and children, dead by the springs, by the mills, by Jideen. The Zionists took their rifles and knocked over their crates of olives. They roared with laughter, their foreign tongues talking over the loudspeakers of mosques and churches: Get your women and children out. Get everybody out.

They planted dynamite under your home in al-Kabri, Baba. Oh, no, you will listen: The rooftop under a fountain of stars where you sat on your father's lap to watch the older kids jump from neighbors' roof to roof. The stairway windows as tall as the cinchona trees. The ten bedrooms with balconies and long delicate arches, each balcony an entry into a family unit within the family unit. The vast, sunny kitchen with wild views of green where your mother used to turn the wild carobs into syrup for your home desserts. The divan washed with water infused with orange blossom where your father met with al-Kabri's elders. The horses, pure-bred with muscle and mane in their stables. Your home, a command post, your land, your name and all it meant once, is gone.

You can stop breathing now,

Mai.

Beirut, December 25, 2002

I wake up the next morning and find visitors from Amman. Amo Jamal's ex-wife, Auntie Shams, is here, sitting in the living room. She's wearing black, but I am colorblind.

I greet her as if I am happy to see her. I ignore all the apprehension in her body, the rattle in her face, what her eyes are trying to tell me. I wish her a Merry Christmas. I tell her all about a trip I recently took with friends to Barcelona. How wonderful I found the architecture, how I couldn't get enough of their marzipan pa—

Mai, habibty. Your father. Nizar is dead.

My world splits. The room fills with gasping shadows. They cram the space, suddenly. So many black bodies. I look up, at nothing, and my teeth clatter. My feet want to defect to elsewhere, to run, to chase him out and out, but they hold me down. They hold the sky up and hold me down.

>Where's Nizar's money? Do you know anything about the money, Mai. Mai?

A group of women cloaked in black enter the room. They beat their chests and flail their arms. They begin to wail. I get up.

Who are you? I ask, pushing everyone off me, who
are you? Get out, get the fuck out.

Amo Jamal holds me back, but I stomp and stomp until
the wailing stops.

They're leaving. Mai, Mai. They left. Nizar's money.
All your father's money. Did he tell you anything? Do you know anything?

I don't. I don't know anything.

I run out of the room. In the corridor, I find Nermin, her
arms wrapped around her body.

Mai, she calls, don't leave me.

I run past her.

Acre, 1948

Jideen was conquered on July 10, 1948 and the Bedouins were evacuated by force. Eventually, only Israeli men took residence in the castle ruins, because the attempt to use its dilapidated rooms by families with women and children failed miserably. The ticks left behind by the herds of goats sheltered by Bedouins during the winter months were carriers of disease. After a month, twenty people fell ill with fever.

The UN partition resolution came a year later. It placed Jideen within the envisaged Arab state rather than the Jewish one, but that didn't matter. Eventually the castle ruins were turned into an Israeli military training camp.

The world is innumerate when it comes to us, Baba. We live, we die, we fall off the grid. We're Lebanese, no Egyptian, no, we're refugees of an alien status, and it doesn't matter. We're anything but who we are. But at least we know basic math. I can tell you that in 1948, 38,183 of us were chased out of al-Kabri and that 1,477 homes were demolished, including yours. Do you know what this means? By proxy, it means that twenty-five of us lived in each home; large, sprawling family homes with big views to our boon. Boisterous homes blasting with song and politics, gossip and argument and laughter and love. Love. Cozy corners that smell like our grandpas and aunties and cousins and siblings, that smell like Acre, like the sea and all the springs and soil of this land. Acre, Baba, it means, unit of land.

Acre, 1948

After al-Kabri's fall, Israelis redirected the springs, Ayn al-'Asal, Ayn al-Mafshuh, Ayn al-Fawar, and Ayn Kabri toward the newly established Kibbutz Kabri up north of the village. I am told the water has a different sound there. It doesn't lull to sleep. What is left of our Garden of Eden now is rubble, dried shrubs, and water-starved weed.

There is one more thing that is left behind. The Haganah's four armored vehicles, two lorries, and one bus, the ones that sparked the battle for our village. The vehicles are an Israeli cenotaph now, painted red, the color of blood. Today, Israeli students are sent on school trips to their site of victory, to witness and commemorate their soldiers' bravery.

Nizar Serhan, Guangzhou, 2000

Faris Serhan

Nana and Nizar's wedding, Cairo, 1969

Nizar, Nermin, and Mai,
Abu Dhabi, 1977

Nermin and Mai, Abu Dhabi, 1981

Nana, Nizar, Nermin, and Mai, Abu Dhabi, 1978

Zeinab Anis, Cairo, 1916

Zeinab Anis and her siblings, Cairo, 1916

Isis Salama, Cairo, 1956

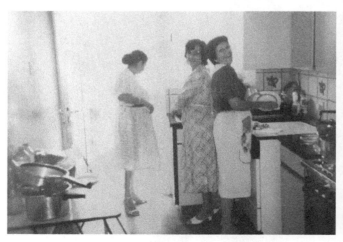
Nadia Serhan and family, Limassol, 1983

Part 2

Beirut, 2002

Malik finds Baba. He makes call after call until he dials +662, he calls Bangkok. He locates him in a hotel room, dead. Malik flies out to bring Baba's body back to Beirut, and I coil in bed in the apartment in Corniche al-Mazra'a for days.

On day three, Auntie Omnia comes over. She knocks on my bedroom door, gently, and hugs me. Her arms reach far, to the edges of my shock, and fold it all back into a warm embrace.

> Pack your bags, she tells me, Nermin and you are coming to stay with me in Hazmieh.

It's Mama's wish, she says.

Our mother has asked for Nermin and me to move. We've seen enough already, she said.

Auntie Omnia is my mother's cousin. She's the Egyptian ambassador to the Arab League in Beirut and her husband, Uncle Magdy, is the dean of the Lebanese International University. Auntie Omnia and Uncle Magdy have three children.

The family is Muslim and Hazmieh is a Christian, French-speaking neighborhood. Beirut, being delineated along sectarian lines, has a colorful and often clashing demographic. It's composed and decomposed of

Christians, Muslim Sunnis, Shiites, Druze, and Armenians, as well as Palestinian refugees. Those still haunted by the war stick to their neighborhoods to this day.

Baba was one of those people. If he were still alive, he would not approve of us staying in Hazmieh. He had personally witnessed the war and how Christian factions had sided with Israel to put an end to the PLO and Palestinian presence in Lebanon. He had witnessed the resulting massacres and the 120 thousand fatalities. But I belong to a different generation and live in a different world twenty years on.

I feel safest in Hazmieh, with Auntie Omnia and her family.

I write my first poem ever and name it *Punch. Delirious. Beirut.*

On the day I put my bags down in front of the building in Hazmieh and look out at the mountains, which the residents of this French-speaking neighborhood call Mont Liban, I write an elegy for a man and his city of youth. I write it to make sense of the losses my father had to endure, those that are now mine, too; to make sense of this sudden and overwhelming feeling that the sky is a roof that is no longer over my head. I ask it questions, but it's intractable and won't answer.

What is father?
Who am I inside his death?
Where did you take him?
Is he really resting now? Because I don't know him to ever rest.

The sky is big, my fist is small, but I punch it anyway. I punch it and punch it and punch it until I become delirious.

Auntie Omnia and Uncle Magdy redefine family. Their love language is crisp. I love you means I love you, though for the most part it's understood without being spoken. It is in the melody of their living pace, the honeycomb texture of their exchange, the no-spaces between them on the couch, the safety of the hours. My gash is big and their care is the gentlest gauze.

Every day, Auntie Omnia asks what Nermin and I would like to eat, ask for the moon, she tells us. Three times a day, Nermin and I join them at the dinner table for a feast of kindness. They love to laugh, to analyze TV series, to be a family, but most of all, they love having us.

Nermin does not drive, so they leave their second car to me. In the evenings, my feet itch, they want to defect to elsewhere. I break loose with nowhere to go. I drive anyway. I blast the car stereo and unbridle myself. Speed through this gorgeous wreck of a city and its everywheres. I break its traffic lights, overtake cars on winding mountains, and zip through blind spots. I cry and cry and cry from Marfa' to Corniche al-Mazra'a and from Ras Beirut to Rmeil, through Hamra, through Rouche, through Achrafieh and Mar Mikhail.

Omnia means wish in Arabic. Late at night, my engine runs out of fuel, and I go back to her.

Is there anything you need, Mai? Ask for the moon.

Cairo, 2002

Nermin and I miss Baba's funeral and fly back to Cairo. My mother wants us with her. We've seen enough already, she keeps saying.

At the arrival hall of Cairo International Airport, I find her waiting. She is wearing black. She runs to hug me, but I don't hug her back.

Why are you wearing black? I ask.
She starts to cry, but crying is ridiculous, he taught me that, so I repeat,

Stop it. Why are you wearing black?

Back home, the phone rings off the hook. People want to come, offer their condolences. I tell them to come in color.

I fly into Cairo with a bag full of my father's remains. The bag contains the following:

1. A Grace Hotel check-in card stamped on December 24, 2002 with his signature. Room 4355. Address: 12 Soi Nana Nuea, Khlong Toei Nuea, Watthana, Bangkok 10110, Thailand.
2. A body ticket on Emirates Airlines by a Teck Hong Kong Funeral Services. The ticket reads BODY REMAINS. LATE: Nizar Faris Serhan. Airport destination: Beirut (Lebanon)
3. Keys, lots of them.
4. Reading glasses.
5. His wristwatch.
6. Chinese catalogs, product samples, and scraps of cloth.
7. His marriage certificate to my mother.
8. Transfer slips to and from the Bank of China. The first worth $2,499,000. The second for $99,630. The third, $1,496,790. The fourth, $73,600. The fifth, $1,996,000. The sixth, $4,298,000.
9. An empty wallet.

Beirut, 2002

Amo Jamal and Malik take charge of washing and burial procedures. I do not dare imagine what takes place in that sterile room, but my dreams show me what I do not want to see: Baba is fifty-seven years old. He is lying still on a flat bed with a white sheet of cloth covering him from the belly button to the knees, his skin still clinging to color, his eyes clouding under his eyelids.

Amo Jamal and Malik wear masks, aprons, and gloves. They remove the morgue's ID tag and the wound dressings. *Bismillah*, they say, before washing him twice with water and a third time with water infused with camphor oil. They remove their gloves, aprons, and masks and throw them in the bin and wear new ones.

They press his stomach gently to expel any remnants, but it is hollow between his bones. They remove the sheet of cloth and wash his private parts. They throw their gloves, aprons, and masks in the bin, prop his head up, and, with a wet Q-tip, clean his nose and nicotine-stained teeth.

They wrap him in a shroud and place him in a casket. They bury him in the Sabra and Shatila Cemetery near Souq al-Hamdieh next to his father, Faris Serhan.

Acre, pre-1948

Imagine your funeral had it been in al-Kabri. I don't see you ever dying young there. I see you staying, living long, carefree, marrying a beautiful Palestinian woman who somehow looks like Nana, having many kids who have many kids, all Palestinian. You would die peacefully, perhaps amidst a reverie, in the only home you've known, amongst family.

I see the whole village coming upon hearing the news, dropping everything, rushing to that home of old Jerusalem stone. The women bringing coffee, rice, sugar, and the shroud. Family and friends from neighboring towns would come too. Your wife in another life passing under your casket three times, and the men letting their beards grow for forty days. In Eid, the Muslim festival of breaking the fast, all of them gathering roses and basil from the fields, making flower bouquets with strings and ribbons to place by your gravestone.

I can never be in that scene I see. I am a child of Palestinian diaspora, a result of a fissure. I am half here, and half with nowhere to go. I am only here because there is no more. You are no more because of a fissure.

Beirut, 2003

I buy a one-way ticket back to Beirut and stay with Auntie Omnia in Hazmieh. The official reason for my visit is to translate the disclaimers of inheritance my aunt and uncles are giving me into Chinese and to authenticate them at the Ministry of Foreign Affairs in preparation for an impending trip back to China. I am also there because I am restless and need to get lost.

Auntie Omnia and her children continue to want to care for me, but I don't want to care for myself. Instead, I hit the night every night, the war architecture, the underground clubs, the acid jazz and baladi music and states of trance. I disappear into nocturnal sounds and float over tables until dawn, until the roof slides open over my head. My head, though, it is sunk between my knees, and I cannot see the sun rising. Strangers lift me up.

Who are you?

Mai.

Mai who?

Never mind.

Do you want to come with us?

Where?

After hours.

I go to strangers' homes and witness strange things, lewd in bathrooms, high on rooftops. I feel sick to my stomach and want to go back home, wherever home is. Instead, I run out and hail a taxi off the street.

Where to?

The Sabra and Shatila Cemetery.

I nod off in the back of a taxi as the sun rises over Beirut. My ears are still whistling with music. The driver parks his car in front of the cemetery and asks if I need help.

Do you have a copy of the Quran?

I have the bible, he says, would that work?

I stumble among tombstones and bouquets of dried-up flowers. Names engraved on marble strike me like death after death. I'm in heels and a slinky dress, the nightclub wristband neon on my wrist. It's a maze of names at distorted angles, and everywhere, cawing. The taxi driver and cemetery guards are following me. They seem concerned.

Can you please leave me alone?

They take a few steps back and stop, watch me from behind a tree. I spin, looking for his name until I spot Serhan. My great grandfather Nayef Serhan, Jeddo Faris Serhan, my father. My father, Nizar Serhan. I try to stand straight, to recite the first verse of *al-Fateha*, but instead, I faint.

Dubai, 2003

I go to Dubai.

I go to Dubai because staring at a mute and immutable sky is madness. Because that freakish foot is mine to bear too. Because I can now that he's gone. I can go anywhere I want, and all I want from this point on is to run toward a vanishing point.

I pull a body off its hanger and wear it. It suits the occasion, this city covered in glitter. I become a copywriter in an international ad agency and rent an apartment on the fiftieth floor of some surreal desert skyscraper. I make friends, runaways like me who work hard and party through the early morning minutes. I pout in photos the way other girls pout. *Drunk, hungover, drunk.* Bleary-eyed in blurry rooms, off limits, I see boys belly dance and give their private parts girl names. I pop the last bottle of champagne at 8 a.m. and by 9 a.m. weep inside my office cubicle. I churn out ads all day, for real estate and banking services and future cars. I chase bad love and break down on the tiled floors of club toilet booths. I buy the slick car of my sleek dreams on loan and shop for designer hats to wear to the horse races.

Ryan Sadler is my Creative Director. I am so grateful to him for landing me my first job in Dubai. No one here would have hired me if he hadn't, not after the mistake I made on my resume. I had spelled copywriter with a space in the middle, copy writer. It's probably why the thirty ad agencies or so I applied to did not hire me. Ryan Sadler must've seen something in me that was worth it, though, that no one else could see.

What that is I have no idea. He negotiates my contract, orders my work permit, and flies me in, but once I start work, he barely finishes a sentence around me.

The office demographic is young, almost everyone is in their twenties. It is made up of Lebanese, Syrian, Indian, Filipino, British, and South African employees. For the most part, those from Lebanon and Syria work in the creative and client-servicing departments, those from India do the below-the-line work, the Filipinos are illustrators, and the white men take up leadership positions.

The agency is a gossip hotbed. Word has it that Faruk, an associate creative director, and Karma, an account manager, are sleeping together. They were caught on ICCTV cameras after office hours. Word has it that Faruk is a sleazebag who keeps a stack of porn magazines in his office desk drawer. Word has it that Samer, an art director, comes from old money in Syria. He invited the team to the family home in Damascus while they shot a TV campaign there. Word has it I shouldn't trust Danni, an Indian copywriter. He loves to gossip, they say. Word has it that, in his heyday, Ryan Sadler won every top advertising award on the planet—the Cannes Lions, the Clio, and the Black Pencil—before he fancied himself a rock star, before cocaine turned him to a crackhead. Washed up, left with a bad rap, and with no agency in London willing to hire him, he came to Dubai, they say.

One month into starting work, I call +20 2, I call my mother in Cairo. I tell her I woke up feeling a gritty sensation in both my eyes, like they were full of sand. I tell her that when I got up to look in the mirror, someone else looked back at me: a monster with crusty eyelashes and eyes the size of ping-pong balls. I tell her, I cannot look myself in the mirror.

My mother tells me she will come to Dubai to take care of me.

Beirut–Dubai

Beirut rings. Amo Jamal wants to know when I intend to go to China. It's been six months. The more we wait, the more the risk of losing everything, he warns.

I have just left the ophthalmologist's clinic where the doctor told me I have a severe case of conjunctivitis, a viral infection caused by pollen or perhaps the chlorine in the piss-warm swimming pool on the top floor of my residential tower. He told me, it's highly contagious, that recovery can take up to one month, that I need to isolate, that it's one of the worst cases of conjunctivitis he has ever seen.

I am in no mood to speak. I tell Amo Jamal, the last time I went to China, I had interpreters, assistants, drivers, and business associates. I had my father and his entourage. What do I know about banks and lawyers, the language, or the streets? I tell him, this whole business is so much bigger than me.

Cairo–Beirut
+961.
Amo Jamal: Alo?
Mama: Alo, Jamal, it's Nana.
Amo Jamal: *Ahlein, Ahlein*. How are you, Nana?
Mama: *Hamdulillah*. Listen Jamal, we have a problem. Nermin is unable to go with Mai to China. Mai is willing to go but cannot handle this responsibility on her own. Is there any way one of her cousins, Fadi or Kamal, can go with her?
Amo Jamal: Oh, let me speak to them and see.

Beirut–Cairo
+20 2
Mama: Alo?
Amo Jamal: *Ahlein*, how are you Nana? Jamal here.
Mama: How are you, Jamal?
Amo Jamal: All is well. Listen, I am very sorry, but both Fadi and Kamal can't take time off work. They said, they can't make it.
Mama: Oh.

Dubai, 2003

I am back in the office. I cannot afford to stay home; I just started this job, and I'm about to apply for leave.

I show up in dark shades, gloves to prevent the spread of my infection, and hand sanitizer to spray over everything I touch.

Ryan walks in looking restless, useless, aware of his uselessness. He asks how I am and gets distracted before I can answer. He hands me a brief for a luxury hotel in Dubai. They need copy for a campaign to promote their five-star restaurants. I get to work.

Faruk shows up in a Hawaiian shirt. He's visibly hungover, his hairy chest exposed halfway down his torso, and his eyes are bloodshot. He takes his place in his cubicle opposite me.

I dreamt of you, he says in a nasal tone.

He says it out loud for the whole room to hear.

Oh yeah, I say, tapping away at my keyboard.

I dreamt of you in a bikini on rollerblades, gliding along Sheikh Zayed Road.

Faruk expects the whole room to be aroused by his dream. I take my shades off.

And was I wearing shades?

Oh, shit, he says, sorry.

I get back to work. I personify French-Asian fusion platters and sex up Moroccan couscous. Ecstasize trite experiences and pour my heart into words I try my hardest to love. Words without meter, or rhyme, or meaning, dressed up cleverly for big spenders. I wax lyric to convince highly stylized people that they don't just want what I sell, but need it. I promise happiness, bigger and better lives, fulfillment, peace of mind, glitter.

My mother arrives in Dubai to mother me. I live in a one-bedroom apartment, and though she helps me clean up my place, buys my groceries, and cooks, I am thankless. I snap at her in the morning before work and in the evening after work. I sit with her and eat the home-cooked meal she prepared in silence. At night, I lie in my bed next to her and dream with my globular eyes open.

She is asleep when a man enters the bedroom. He stops at the foot of my bed, and he's all teeth and muscle and grime. He is darker than everything around him, as if the light Mama had left on in the kitchen doesn't fall on him. He starts to wrap a big iron chain around his fist, his face twisting with tears. I realize, somehow, I am the perpetrator of his pain, but for the life of me, I don't know what I've done. He raises his chained arm high up to whip me.

Who are you? What are you doing here? I want to say. I try to open my mouth, to scream. I try to lift my arms up to shield my head, but my muscles are paralyzed. Time is warped, it could be anywhere between an eternity and a minute. Then, suddenly, release. The next thing I know, I am slashing the air with a pillow—but the man is gone.

Mama holds me close. She squeezes me tight.

Beirut–Dubai

+971

Mai: Hello?

Amo Jamal: Mai, *habibti*, how are you?

Mai: I'm good Amo, how are you?

Amo Jamal: I have great news. You won't be going to China alone.

Mai: Who's coming?

Amo Jamal: Malik, God bless him. He is the best person for this task. He's worked with Nizar. He knows more than anyone about the business. He's offered to go with you.

I hit a beach bar with friends on the weekend. They don't believe in t-shirt and jeans in Dubai. Everyone gets dolled up, and so, so do I. At the bar, my friends and I down tequila shots. I need it to speak the language of this city. To cut loose, to catch the roving eyes of other runaways, to run to the dance floor and shake off my troubles. On the dance floor, I close my eyes, become the beat, convince myself I'm so in love with everything and everything loves me back.

I dance and feel an arm snake its way around my waist. Sense someone's sweat on my back. I turn to look and it's Faruk. I remove his hand and keep on dancing, but Faruk has conjured me up in his wet dreams for nights as a bikini-clad chick in rollerblades, gliding up and down Sheikh Zayed Road.

Ryan is here, he shouts over the music, all over my neck.

I look over Faruk's shoulder and find Ryan by the bar, all eyes on me, as awkward in his own skin as ever.

He likes you, he says.

Ha?

Ryan, that fool.

Fool? He's your friend.

Are you listening? I just said he likes you.

I leave the dance floor. Faruk follows.

Why are you telling me this?

Well, it's the truth, he says sliding a hand around my waist.

Don't touch me.

Easy now.

I push him away.

You think you were hired cause you're good? he says, ha, you're just a hot chick he hired to look at.

My mother leaves. She leaves because she's tired of me snapping at her, of my breath reeking of alcohol, of silence over dinner, of never being present even when I am there. She leaves because even though my eyes are now clear, my boundaries are all blurred.

Mama leaves in tears.

Dubai, 2003

Mehrzad is Iranian, nineteen years old or so. I meet him several times in after-hour parties, gatherings that take place in dark and loud dens. Night after night, I watch him sit like a racecar, parked. I watch him rev, impatient legs whooshing from room to room. I don't know what he does for a living in Dubai, but I can tell whatever it is is a hustle. He's always biting his nails, always whispering in people's ears and disappearing behind closed doors. Sometimes we speak and I notice his chiseled boy-face, the tyranny in his talk. I do not always look into his eyes because when I do, I see danger, how they do not reflect the light.

He calls me one day, he calls to say he's got something important to tell me, and could he please come over to speak in private?

Merzhad sits and he's already in a hurry. He cracks his knuckles as I sit down. He has confidential information, he says. He tells me I can't share it with anyone. He moves closer to me on the couch and his voice drops a notch.

I'm an informer, he tells me, I work for the Criminal Investigation Department, the CID.
He tells me he's found a file on me, and that he's read it.

What have I done?

They know about you.

About what?

The after-parties, he says, the drugs.

What drugs? No, no, no. I don't do drugs.

Well, that's not what's in the file. They have your name. You might get deported.

Mehrzad tells me he can get me out of this. He can get me out of this if I go down with him now to the ATM machine and hand him all the money in my bank account.

I go down with him. There is no gun to my back, but there might as well be. I put my debit card in and punch my password while he looks on. The machine whirrs, counts the bills. I give him all I have: AED 10,000. I give him my food, electricity bill, and gas for the rest of the month.

What is this? Where's the rest of it?

That's all I have.

Liar.

I swear, I say, I swear to God, it's all I have.

He stuffs the cash in his pocket and, before he leaves, warns me again.

Remember, if you tell anyone about this—I'll be watching you.

I watch Merzhad run, whoosh toward a vanishing point.

Baba, I'm like you in more ways than I'd like to think. All my life I've been playing games to survive. I've developed techniques to survive almost to a fault.

People's perception is limited by what is possible, but I have endured some of the impossible, and my sensors have had to adapt to extremes. I can now listen at frequencies beyond the ordinary hearing range. Detect what people's bodies emit when they're not talking. Early on, I've learnt the power of words. How they can ricochet or set fire to a minute or many lifetimes. I've learnt how to run fast so my past doesn't catch up with me, how to locate changes in my flight, find my way in the dark. I laugh when a situation calls on me to scream, erect the highest barriers to protect this big and brittle heart. I know how to charm, Baba, I knew how to diffuse your rage with a smile. I can detect danger, the smell of a burning tree 100 miles away. I breathe the genes of my ancestors 100 years away.

You know, for all the times I've survived, Baba, I was only trying to survive you.

Dubai, 2003

I walk through the departure gate at Dubai International Airport and head straight to the flight schedule display. Malik has flown in from Beirut to meet me and is here in Dubai. I am supposed to find him at Costa Coffee, past the check-in, but first I have to figure out the first stop in what is a long route from Dubai to Bahrain to Singapore to Bangkok to Hong Kong, and from Hong Kong by train to Shenzhen. I stop at the flight information display, find my bearings, check in my luggage, then head to our meeting point.

In the café, I spot him before he spots me. He is as handsome as ever in a corner table. I pretend not to see him and stand in the queue to order my coffee. He waves at me without calling my name, a remnant of intimidation from the bygone days of Baba, of course. I ignore him. I want him to call out my name, to set new rules. He waves again, then, finally:

Mai!

I walk up to him sensing the elephant in the room, that the obstacle between us has been lifted, and that I am now some kind of prized acquisition placed placidly on his path. I am prepared for this. I have packed accordingly, nothing too revealing or inviting. In fact, I am boyish in my checkered shirt with rolled up sleeves, my loose jeans and worn-out Converse. I walk up to him with just enough of a smile to convey courtesy and fix his eyes with my gaze to stop them from moving anywhere else on me. He gets up and I shake his hand, firmly.

After a flurry of hellos, condolences, the great loss, and waxing lyric about Baba and what he meant to him, we sit down for coffee. We sit down in a different world and tables turning, no watchtower over our heads. Me, a tired renegade, and him, still an alien to me of unknown origins. All I know about Malik is that he was my father's right-hand man during the last year of his life. He will know his way around all the towns in China, he will hire translators, lawyers if need be, he will book hotels and transportation, he's tapped into my father's networks, he has leads, he might even have been a confidante, if such person ever existed.

Some small talk and then I notice Malik getting shifty. His body is trying to acquire more space on a small table for two, to get comfortable, but I am sitting straight with my coffee close to my chest, my hands wrapped around the mug.

What's wrong? I ask.

Just tired, he says, I had a big night.

I don't ask him about his big night, so he repeats,

I had a big night, last night.

I notice the wedding band on his finger.

Oh yeah.

Woah, what a night.

I scoop the foam out of my latte, place it on the small white plate, and take a sip.

How are your wife and kids? I ask.

My wife?

Show me a photo of your kids.

144

Malik opens his wallet and pulls out a polaroid of his family.

    She's beautiful, I say of his wife, what's her name?

    Suha, he says, the name forming a dull ring in his mouth.

    God bless, I say.

Malik shifts in his chair, rubs his neck, then says,

    No one is beautiful after seven years of marriage.

I attempt a laugh, but it fizzles quickly into a sigh.

    Haven't you heard of the seven-year itch?

    No idea, I say taking another sip.

    You know, you have a lot of Nizar.

    You think?

    Yeah, the way your gaze—Nizar, he never looked up. He read people, but didn't want anyone to read him.

I look up at him.

    What was it that you did last night? I ask.

    He was a real rebel, your dad, he continues.

I nod, pretending to know what he's referring to.

    I was with another woman, he says.

    Other than your wife?

    Yes.

I get up.

    Where are you going?

    Excuse me. Will be right back.

I have an ancestral tick. When boundaries blur, I slip elsewhere. When I feel the heat of words, I run through fire escapes. But sometimes, I don't make it out in time, and my gut catches fire.

It's gotten worse recently. The fireball rolls down my body, my back, my legs, and I break into sweat. My body coils around itself the way heat curls paper. I went to see a doctor about it and he said it's IBS or, in my case, grief sounding its horn.

I walk to where the toilets are only because I'm so cramped, I cannot run. I keep the toilet seat down and sit, hugging my knees close to my chest. Time drags while I wait for my insides to unclench. I look inward, try to find my way out of a vast dark. Malik rings me. I silence the phone. He rings again and again. The silent rings vibrate, ram me, flare everything up. I don't answer.

Time passes and the pain subsides. I pick myself up, wash my face and hands, walk out. I find him right there by the toilets.

We're late, they're calling for our flight.

I walk past him.

You know cheating on your wife, that's not good, I say.

Bahrain, 2003

We land in Bahrain for a three-hour layover before our next stop in Singapore. We head to a café and sit.

What is the plan when we get to Shenzhen? I ask.

The plan is to meet Abu Hazem.

Who is Abu Hazem?

You don't know Abu Hazem?

Should I?

Well, he was your father's business partner in Shenzhen.

He never mentioned him.

That's Nizar for you, he says, laughing, Abu Hazem is your main source for all your father's business transactions, assets, and possibly accounts too.

Can I trust him?

Malik leans forward, lights a cigarette and offers me one. I take it. He lights it for me.

You can't trust anyone, he says, look, there's a lot of money at stake. He will naturally look after his own interests. That's why I need you to be quiet and leave the talking to me.

To you? You just said I can't trust anyone.

He smiles.

God, you're just like him.

Singapore, 2003

We land in Singapore Changi Airport after an eight-hour flight and a dream just as long.

I dream of a frail man moving across a small room that is half world, half the color morgue. Ash skin and an oversized jacket on crumbling shoulders. He is not angry, he is cold. The cold has broken him, and all the blankets in the world won't warm his bones. The room is dim with walls that cave in, and an armchair, and an electric heater burning orange on the floor. The frail man is looking at me, but he won't speak. His eyes are telling me something his mouth won't say. He is okay with it, not speaking, but his eyes still tell me something happened, something broke all the words. Who knows, whatever signals he is giving me are incomplete. He sits down in the armchair near the heater and wraps himself in blanket over blanket.

I wake up from my dream not knowing where I am until I find my head on Malik's shoulder. I turn my whole body the other way, coil into myself.

Bangkok, 2003

We touch down in Bangkok, a city I have never been to yet somehow is now bound to me forever. It is many things to many people and a black box to me. It is the final hours, alone in some three-star hotel where time stopped.

I want to sit with this terminus for a minute, the last hours. What happened? What made him check into a hotel rather than a hospital if he couldn't fly anymore? The death certificate cites the cause of death as a heart attack, but Baba's heart was fine. The little I know is that his lungs had filled up with water. Pneumonia, perhaps, a shortness of breath, a cold numbness. Perhaps there was no doctor on the flight to advise him to check into a hospital. Perhaps no one spoke his language.

We have a five-hour layover in Bangkok. I spot a row of computer stations and tell Malik I need to go check for work emails.

I type in Grace Hotel, 12 Soi Nana Nuea, Khlong Toei Nuea, Watthana, Bangkok 10110, Thailand. The hotel that appears is white and ribbed with pothole-like windows. It's nice enough to have a website, and that eases something in me. But then I click on its location on the map and find out something else, that the hotel is a twenty-minute commute by car from the airport.

I'm lost. For my father to have decided to discontinue his journey, he must've been in critical condition. He was in critical condition, I know that, because he was found dead in his hotel room shortly after checking in. Why did he pick a hotel that was so far from the airport? Was anyone with him? Who?

～♪

> Malik, I say sitting next to him in the airport lounge, when you came to Bangkok to bring the body back, what did you find out about what happened?
>
> They told me he screamed for help and by the time someone ran to his hotel room, he was already gone.
>
> Did you find any money on him?
>
> No, nothing.
>
> But isn't that weird? He had big bundles of cash on him all the time, never a wallet or a credit card.
>
> There was no money. All his belongings have been returned to you.
>
> But he was going from the airport straight to the hospital. Does he have a bank account in Beirut?
>
> I don't know.
>
> Malik.
>
> What?
>
> Malik.
>
> Yes?
>
> That money was stolen.

Hong Kong, 2003

We pass through Hong Kong immigration and cross the bridge over the Sham Chun River, the natural border between Hong Kong and mainland China. We purchase an Octopus Card to catch a train up north to Shenzhen. On the train, scenes of the Victoria Harbor, fallow fields, and fish ponds swish backwards. Malik tells me he's booked rooms on separate floors.

Why? I ask, regretting it immediately.

Why do you think?

I don't think anything.

You're a big girl, he says, you can figure it out.

So, who are we meeting, anyone other than Abu Hazem? Will we be seeing Ou?

Yes, we must. She's in Yiwu.

I remember Baba introducing me to a woman in Guangzhou. A business woman, very pretty. She seemed close to him.

Lin.

Lin, yes.

Why do you keep doing this?

What?

Changing the subject.

Shenzhen, 2003

By the time we get to China, Malik's good looks lose all their appeal. He's married, with kids, and even if he wasn't, his timing stinks of sleaze, of exploitation. He's trying to take advantage of me, clearly.

I realize I will have the added responsibility of managing him and his expectations on this trip. I will have to play mouse to his cat, dumb myself before his innuendos, reject him without making him feel dejected, placate him so he stays firmly on my side, and try to gauge what exactly he expected when he signed up to accompany me on this trip.

But for now, I'm hungry, and have learned my lessons trying to order without understanding. I bring it up with Malik.

>Ah, Shenzhen has changed a lot since you've last been here, he says, how about fresh seafood?

>No, not feeling it.

>OK, a few Arab restaurants have opened too. There's a new Lebanese one. The owner is a good friend of Nizar. You wanna try it out?

The Lebanese restaurant is on a wide and busy street, not in some dingy backside alley like the halal joints of my last trip. It's in the style of *A Thousand and One Nights*;

dim with coffered ceilings, chandeliers beaded in red, plush pillows, and openwork lights that play off shadows on the walls. We go up to the second floor, a trail of incense following us up the wooden stairs. I get to the landing and a tall man on my left turns to look at me then rises slowly to his feet. He looks stunned to see me.

Nizar's daughter?

Yes, I say, how do you know?

The man comes closer, eyes wide like he's just seen a ghost.

> I don't know, I just—it's the strangest thing, he says, I just felt his presence the moment you walked in. Welcome. I'm Rabeh, a good friend of your father's.

A massive tray of mezzah appears shortly after with green and black olives, *batata harra*, *baba ghanoush*, *tabbouleh*, *kibbeh*, and stuffed grape leaves. Malik and I are guests of honor, it seems, and everyone is waiting on us hand and foot. Rabeh though, he's just happy looking at me and summoning his late friend's spirit.

> How I miss that man, *ya Allah*. You know, he had all his meals here when he was in Shenzhen, many of his meetings too. Palestinians, Syrians, Iraqis, Lebanese, he brought them all here. You see that corner over there with the round table? That was his spot.

I look behind me at the round table. I see Baba there, slouched in a remake of some designer brand, his brain computing under turned-down eyelids, thinking shipments, containers, contracts, filling up ashtrays with cigarette butts.

> He was a chain-smoker, your father, you know, burning the candle from both ends really, Rabeh says. I told him, when he came back after that thing with his foot. I told him he was working too hard, that he should quit and move to Beirut.
>
> I know, I say, tired.
>
> He was disappointed when you left, he continues, but I understand. I mean, a girl like you has no business being in China.

I stop eating and look at Malik for the first time since we sat down. His eyes are on me. They've been on me the whole time, it seems.

> But, what can I say, Rabeh continues, Nizar was the first Arab businessman to come here. He built an empire out of nothing.
>
> Nizar was a pioneer, Malik says to me, you'll see when we meet other traders. They all have his picture framed above their desks.

Platters of lamb chops, shish taouk, and kebab to feed a whole village arrive. Malik digs in.

> Like *The Godfather*, I say.
>
> Oh, he was a proud father, Rabeh continues, missing the reference. You know he carried photos of you and your sister in his shirt pockets. He used to show them to us all the time.

Back in my hotel room, I disconnect my hotel telephone line and take a long nap. It's dark when I wake up, but this young coastal city that is tall by design is so lit. Everything outside my window twinkles. It startles me into wakefulness. Shenzhen has changed its skin fast.

Not so long ago, it was a sleepy fishing village, not so long ago I couldn't walk down the street without feeling like a spectacle, not so long ago, Baba was here. Now Lebanese restaurants are cropping up next to coffeehouses and sprawling technology markets on the high streets, now the mountains are being leveled for more and more development. I search for Baba's traces in other windows, on the bay's surface, but this place is almost beyond recognition. I connect the cable back to the phone and it rings immediately. Malik wants me to get ready for our meeting with Abu Hazem.

This is no place fit for the makings of a business tycoon or an empire. This is a low-rise on a narrow alleyway where buildings are stuck so close to each other, neighbors can lean out of windows and shake hands. I walk up a crumbling staircase under a flickering white light to the second floor. Malik rings the doorbell.

    Wait. Is this Baba's office?
    Yes.
    Whatever happened to the one I stayed in, on the thirty-third floor?
    Nizar had many businesses, Mai, and more than one office.
    Is Abu Hazem his partner in this office?
    Yes, listen. He will play dumb. He will pretend there are no outstanding balances with clients, that he knows nothing. Leave the talk to me.
    I want to go to the other office, I tell him, the one I stayed in.
Malik rings the doorbell.

Abu Hazem opens. I recognize him, his oval face, his green bulging eyes, his thin lips, the potbelly. He is one of the traders who had joined us once for dinner, one of those men who crammed on Baba's side of the dinner table. He shakes Malik's hand.

Ya hala, ya hala, he says to me.

He lets us in. The space is shabby and stripped of everything but function. Odd pieces of furniture are thrown together with no regard for taste. Holes in the walls make way for electricity cables that hang across. Florescent white ceiling lights flicker next to bare yellow bulbs, a cracked black leather couch and a desk chair, a floral oil cloth curtain half off its rail, files on the shelves, and an outmoded IBM computer.

He takes his place behind the desk, under Baba's picture frame. The picture is blown up to a blur, pixelated. He's a frail man in it, staring suspiciously at the camera. His sunken cheeks have changed the shape of his head and enlarged all his features. It's a recent picture, and I cannot help but think of his missing foot somewhere there under the frame.

I was told again not to speak, to leave the talking to Malik, the man in my company. But I'm watching Malik and finding his strategy soft and his words off putting. He's hunched toward Abu Hazem, body in appeal.

> Nizar left two daughters, he begins, no sons. You
> have daughters yourself, Abu Hazem. You know
> how it is. We need to help them.

Abu Hazem clasps the arms of his chair with both hands. He swings left and right, but his face is stern, and I can already tell that if he has information, he will not share it with us.

Nizar didn't trust anybody with his money, he says.

But you were his partner here, Malik says, didn't
you have a joint bank account, at least for your
company?

You're asking me? You were his closest confidante.
Do *you* know anything about his finances?

I get up and look around the room, wander into other
rooms and disappear, slamming doors behind me. When
I return, I slip behind Abu Hazem's desk chair and open
the window. I stay there a while. I want him to feel me
there, to cause a discomfort.

I know enough to know you—

The answer is no, Abu Hazim says, we kept our
accounts separate.

Come on, Abu Hazem, Malik says.

Excuse me, if his own daughter doesn't know, how
should I?

I slip past Abu Hazem toward the shelves, pull a folder
out and pretend to flip through its contents. Big figures
jump out of invoices and contracts—four digits, five, six.
I rip one invoice out and pick a green marker from a
mug in front of Abu Hazem. I circle the sum total.

What about this? I ask.

What about it? he says, looking at Malik.

But Malik is looking at me. His eyes are telling me to be
quiet, to sit down.

You made a lot of money working for Baba, didn't
you?

Listen, he tells me, whatever you heard of your
father's fortune is an exaggeration. Our com-
mission was ten percent on every deal, split
between us.

>Yes, but he also opened a factory in the last year, I say, he made 100 percent profit on those deals.
>That factory is in Yiwu, he says, go ask Ou about it.
>What about this office?

Abu Hazem laughs.

>What about it? It's worth nothing, a rental. You want these chairs and tables?

I spot Malik in the hotel restaurant the next morning, and I'm in no mood to speak. The way he handled Abu Hazem last night doesn't sit well with me. I head to the breakfast buffet before heading to his table. I decide to try something new. I serve myself mangosteen and monk fruit, then head to where he sits. I have never tried mangosteen before. He watches me stare at the fruit, not knowing how to open it.

>Do you need help with this?
>No, I say, knocking on the hard fruit shell with a teaspoon.
>You need a serrated knife, he says, let me help.
>No. Listen, do you remember Hongxi, Baba's translator?
>Oh, yes, Hongxi. He lives in Shenzhen.
>Right. I want him to come with us to Yiwu.
>Why, we don't need him.
>I do.

Malik picks up his pace to catch up with me by the entrance of Baba's Shenzhen office apartment. We get into the elevator and hit the thirty-third-floor button. As the doors shut, a Chinese woman slips one lacquered hand through and pushes the doors back open.

She's wearing a silk shirt with a tight miniskirt, high heels, and her long black hair is down to her waist. Malik's eyes rove over her body. The ride feels like ground floor to eternity.

On the thirty-third floor, I pull out a bundle of keys and try them out until the lock on Baba's office apartment finally clicks open. I enter and feel paradox after paradox. Last time I was here, life was half-lived in this space, a life of short stops, canned food, windows that do not open, and a man running on reserve. Today this man is gone and what remains fools one into thinking he's just gone for a walk, and will return soon. The shoes next to the door ready to go, two cups in the sink with coffee ground patterns that suggest a future, the heat of that slap still warm on my cheek, my howls as I tore this place down, his pleas, his apologies.

I notice no one's probably been here since he last left. In the bathroom, I find his beard hair in the sink and run the water to wash it down the drain. I stand in the middle of his office space and look out at the city. The sun is shining over buildings that cut through the sky like brilliant shards of glass. Yet for the life of me, I cannot find what I'm looking for. More invoices, business cards, transfer slips, and fabric samples on the desk. Files upon files on the shelves. I bring a pile down and search for clues. What am I looking for?

What am I looking for? I ask Malik.

Guangzhou, 2003

The next day, we fly to Guangzhou to meet with Lin. Malik brings a translator I don't know to the meeting. He's upbeat in the taxi, hopeful. Lin was by his side in hospital during his final days. Malik believes she will impart some essential information. Or so he wants me to believe.

We enter the marketplace and pull up by her shop where the same sight awaits me: men sipping their black beers, people-watching while their children run about their legs.

Lin hasn't changed either, she's as beautiful as I last saw her. She's surrounded by her female coworkers, as usual, when she greets us at the entrance. The pink flush in her cheeks tells me she's nervous about seeing me, the flare of her lip tells me she has a lot to say. I wish I could talk to her directly, in private. Instead, I squeeze her shoulder and hope my fondness translates. I let her lead us upstairs to the same rectangular table we once sat around with Baba. Lin and I sit on opposite sides and the green tea arrives in small porcelain cups. Malik starts the conversation.

> Lin, you were one of the closest people to Nizar. You know, being all the way here in China, his daughters don't know much about his finances or how he ran his business.

The interpreter translates. Lin's response is the same one I have heard from Malik and Abu Hazem. Baba didn't trust anyone when it came to money.

But you know he had lots of it, he says.

You were with him in hospital? I interrupt.

是, she nods.

What happened? Why was he sick?

She starts to recount the last days in Chinese. She holds her temples, her chest, she hugs her shoulders, she sighs. She points at me. The interpreter translates:

> He was here in Guangzhou. It started with flu-like symptoms. He had a forty-degree fever, chills, muscle aches, a terrible headache. His secretary called Lin and said she didn't know what to do. So Lin drove to his hotel, found him in bad shape, unable to breathe. She checked him into the International SOS Clinic. The next day, he developed a dry cough and his lungs filled with water.

Pneumonia? I ask.

肺炎?

The translator tells me it might have been, that soon after my father had to be put on a mechanical ventilator. His lungs—

> I object. I spoke to him, I say, I spoke to him and he sounded fine, he sounded strong. He told me not to believe any of it, to book a ticket to Beirut. He said it was okay for him to travel.

The room falls silent. Eventually, Lin resumes. She hugs her shoulders again, points at me.

> He was in critical condition, the interpreter carries on, she's saying Ou called you and told you so.

What was Ou doing in Guangzhou?
她在广州做什么?

Lin, did Nizar mention anything about his bank accounts? Malik asks. Did he make any transfers during that time?

What was Ou doing here? I interrupt.
歐在廣州做什麼?

Your father called Ms. Ou, they tell me. He asked her to come.

Lin gets up and begins to move around the room. She is describing a frail man. He was cold, she tells me, so cold that all the blankets they wrapped him in could not warm his bones.

This can't be true, I tell them, I tell the whole room.

He was pretending. He wanted to leave the hospital at any cost, to see you and your sister.

Lin pretends to rip something off her arms. The interpreter continues,

The doctors told him if he got on a plane, he wouldn't make it, but your father wouldn't listen to anyone. He ripped all the tubes and walked off. He wouldn't listen.

Lin tells me he might've sounded strong on the phone, but she was with him. When he hung up with you, she says, he was crying. But crying is ridiculous, I tell myself.

Where is Hongxi? I scream, I told you to call him!

Malik opens the back door of the taxi for me.

I'm walking, I say.

You want me to come with you?

No.

He follows me down Wenming Road toward Da'nan Road, up Guangzhouqiyi Road and toward the street-food sellers on Beijing Road. Here, hundreds of cramped stalls abound and food sellers flock before woks, hotpots, bamboo steamer baskets full of soft xia jiao and bao, and pit barrels that foam with gutter oil and fizz with blistering skin. People lean on cages stacked one on top of the other, and inside the cages, the half-alive and feathered await their turn to become all-dead.

My guts turn, it's another bout of IBS, but I cannot stop here, so I run, I run against pains that shoot up my shoulder and down my legs. I will my stomach cramps into submission. I want to go home, is all I can think, wherever the fuck home is.

I'm too tired after, but there are people who want to see me. I tell Malik, I'm not leaving the hotel tonight, so they come over and meet us in the reception. An all-male Levantine band shows up; resident Syrian traders, Jordanian agents, Lebanese and Palestinian visiting businessmen. This time, though, they're at ease around me, curious, shameless. My father is no longer here to keep them in check or segregate the space. I find myself sitting in the center. They gather. They have stories they're eager to share, lots of stories, and I am torn between fact and fiction. They tell me my father was a millionaire, no, a billionaire. They argue, raise their arms and voices, throw figures and estimates of fortune. I should check offshore accounts, they say, in Lebanon, no Macau, no, in Switzerland. No, no, Nizar didn't have as much as he led everyone to believe. If he had he would've spent it, and he wasn't a spender. No one knows, he kept those things secret. What are you talking about, brother? He had businesses all over Southeast China, from Hong Kong to Shanghai, the factory, the trips to Macau every weekend.

Macau? I interrupt, then I remember his passport, a palimpsest of stamps. Macau many times over. Where is that place?

Macau, Mai, Malik tells me, The Vegas of China.

You mean a gambling town?

Among other things, he says and turns to grin at the men in our company.

What? Just say it. He's not here anymore.

The men shift in place, their eyes deliberating how much to disclose to his daughter, a young woman, the only woman amongst them. Finally, Malik draws a deep breath.

Prostitutes, he says.

I listen without moving a muscle, without betraying a thought, and they talk and talk about one of the wealthiest cities in the world and its underbelly. How gambling revenues are five times that of Vegas, about casinos, brothels, and exotic encounters. They tell me my father was a womanizer of the first order. He had charm, humor. Women flocked around him. Women he found on sidewalks, in massage parlors, saunas, nightclubs, luxury malls, hotel receptions. Sex workers who stood under neon-lit monuments, before his big cars.

Malik brims. He's watching my reaction, waiting for me to crack. There's an invitation here, I am aware. I am being asked to engage in a world of fetishes and fantasies. He wants me to relent and finally admit I know what *fucking* means. He's getting a kick out of our audience, all this testosterone surrounding me. I don't. I don't give him the satisfaction, until a word is thrown in, a name, and its flames burn me. Somebody mentions Ou.

> What about her? I ask.
> She was okay with all of it, they say.
> Who is she to have a say? I laugh.
> Oh. You don't know.
> Don't know what?
> Ou was his mistress. Of five years.

My head on a pillow and a film reel running shadows on the wall:

Limassol:
My uncle's wife   Auntie Shams
topless poolside   The Essex Hotel
A Palestinian version of Monica Bellucci
All curves and eyes like guns
The man I know as father enters   Sees her
Breasts bare   oiled up in coconut
war undone inside him   He calls her a whore
the women scram.

Cairo:
The man I call Father finds out   Nermin has a boyfriend
He follows them to a restaurant   Sees a red rose   A boy
Storms in   He yanks her off her chair.

Beirut:
I make a friend   We lark in bookshops
Watch a play   Find hidden city gems
I tell the man I call Father to join us   Have coffee with us
He does so   He comes to interrogate him
To intimidate him   Friend never calls again.

Yiwu:
A toy market   Khaled, me and Ou
Ou observing us   Ou, the next day
telling her man   my father something
I do not know   Next thing I know
I'm again forbidden.

Cairo:
Mama warning us   Baba plans to tap the landline
Careful with who you call   What you say
Your girl-to-girl secrets.

Rounds of Monopoly   money, property
always the win   Advance to Go
collect two hundred.

Ou again   My dream of Ou
Titi's Cairo closet, emptied
Tiny dresses Ou had sewn on a dead night
Titi sleeping tight.

I stitch story after story until the man I call Father comes
undone. Who was he?

I stitch story after story until the plot rips. I snag the tip of a thread. That time in Beirut after Amo Nabil passed away. Baba called me to the side and told me something I immediately unheard—

Two passcodes, he said, two bank accounts: Nermin's birthday and your birthday.

The next morning, I wait for Malik in the all-you-can-eat hotel restaurant with no desire to eat anything at all. I have a lot to tell him. I also need to tell him off. He walks in with bags under his eyes.

Didn't sleep? I ask.
Up all night.
Me too.
Oh, ha! You must've heard all the banging and screaming then.
No, I didn't.
How come? We were so loud.
A fight? I ask.
A fight?

I want to laugh at the way he's looking at me, his eyes and mouth un-forming. Instead, I stop fiddling with cups and spoons and sit squarely in my seat, staring back.

You know what, I understand you, Mai, he says.
What's there not to understand?
I'm calling your bluff.
What bluff?
You pretend to be so innocent, like you don't understand.
Well, I'm calling your bluff too, I say.
I need another coffee.

He pours himself another coffee, and I wait for him to take the first sip before I begin to speak.

I want Hongxi to come with us to Yiwu, Malik.

Okay.

And why didn't you tell me about Ou?

Yiwu, 2003

We take off in a rainstorm, to Yiwu. The flight is bumpy. Through the drizzle on my window, I see a vast mountain range wrapped in a haze thick as cotton. The seat belt signs remain on long after our ascent through eddies of air. I want to ask for a cup of water, but all the cabin crew are strapped and jig-jogging in their seats. I look at Malik and find his eyes and fists clenched. He's mumbling something under his breath, presumably verses from the Quran to calm himself down.

Why didn't you tell me about Baba and Ou, Malik? I ask.

He doesn't answer. We hit a rough patch, more turbulence, and I jolt toward him.

Why didn't you tell me about Ou?

Because we need her, Mai. Okay? We need her.

Who is *we*?

I'm innumerate, Baba. I presume love equals loyalty. That a man receives royalties, from love and loyalty, long after the bankroll stops. A million and one good deeds for free. But most people love unequally, economically. Remember Shenzhen, how the traders swarmed around you like moths around light? They kept me invisible for a price. Now look at me, alleged heiress, how they swarm, surround me, alleging wild things about you. Remember Guangzhou, how Lin's girls fluttered around you like harpies? I stared at you hard that day, tried to understand what exactly about your bald head or sagged skin amounted to desire. Then there is Malik who embezzles facts, who's prepared to pay any price, it seems, to undress me. He calls that loyalty. They tell me, Ou served you the longest, which means she raked in the most. I tell you now, you were right about a lot of things and wrong about one. You should've never trusted Ou.

Yiwu, 2003

Hongxi greets us in the arrivals hall. The three of us hail a cab and head to Baba's Yiwu apartment. In the elevator, Malik reminds me to be nice. Ou has lived with Baba in this apartment for five years, he tells me. She will have nowhere to go. She might have access to his bank accounts. She will perceive me as a threat. She will need to be placated. He rings the doorbell. She opens, finds three people, guests as it were, and proceeds to act as if she's receiving two. She welcomes Malik and Hongxi in, invites them to sit in the living room.

What you would like to drink? she asks.

Ou is wearing a cream vest made of premium grade wool. She's wearing a delicate gold bracelet on her wrist. Her legs are long and elegant in sheer stockings. Legs that once laid next to my father in bed, that wrapped around him. I find the thought disgusting.

Coffee please, Malik says, thanks Ou.

She busies herself in the kitchen and comes back with Turkish coffee for two, puts one before Malik, the other before Hongxi. Malik blows in his cup while Hongxi looks at me apologetically. He does not touch his coffee.

It was Nizar's coffee, she tells Malik, I only serve for his friend now.

I get up, head to the bedroom and lock the door from the inside. There is a picture frame by the bed. Baba is stick thin with a loafer on his left foot and a slipper on his amputated right foot. Ou wears a smile for what appears to be the very first time. Or it might be that she's just never smiled in my presence. Baba is caught off guard by the camera lens. He's mid-movement, mid-sentence. Ou, however, is ready for her shot.

She knocks on the door.

Open now please, she says.

I ignore her. Open drawers, scan the shelves, slide the door to his closet open. His trousers are neatly hung and his shirts are folded on the shelves, still. Ou knocks harder.

Mai, open.

I get a pair of his pajamas out and sit on the bed. I inhale. The pajamas still carry his heat, his hurry, his smoke. I inhale until I can no longer fathom the difference between what is here and what is gone, until this loss steams my face, and the tears come, like a tidal wave.

Mai, open the door.

I grab a suitcase from under the bed and empty its contents, Chinese catalogs, product samples, and scraps of cloth. In the inside pocket, I find two bank transfer slips from the Bank of China, Yiwu branch, one worth $64,000, the another worth $115,000. I slip them back into place and begin to empty the contents of his cupboards. I pack his shirts, trousers, pajamas. I pack his eau de cologne. I open the door.

What are you doing? Malik asks.

What is in this suitcase, Ou asks, trying to grab the handle.

>This is my father's apartment. I am terminating the lease. End of this month is when you're out, I want to say.

Instead, I make a run toward the door, down the stairs, the suitcase banging its way down with me.

I need a straight line from A to B. I don't want secrets lurking behind trees or fictions fogging the way, or ghost whispers. I want to leave all the shadows behind so nothing darks me.

I turn my phone on in the morning after a night of silence.

"Where did you go?"
                    3:42 p.m.
"Are you OK?"
                    3:50 p.m.
"Dinner?"
                    7:15 p.m.
"Hey."
     11:58 p.m.

I call him. He's out somewhere with loud music in the background; a bar or night club. I tell him I am going to The Bank of China without him tomorrow morning. All I want is Hongxi, please, 9 a.m.

You left Ou in hysterics, Mai.

Please, she is not—Hongxi at 9 p.m. Please, OK?

In my bag is Baba's passport and mine, his death certificate, the family civil registration document, the disclaimers of inheritance, and some bank transfer slips. I meet Hongxi in front of The Bank of China. We walk in and head to the customer service desk. I ask him to explain the situation to the man there. The man examines all the documents and excuses himself. When he comes back, he asks us to wait a few minutes. The manager will be with us shortly, he says.

A few minutes later, the bank manager emerges. He's a friendly man with a spring in his step. No fluff, no drumroll there. He shakes my hand firmly and I shake his with equal force. He ushers us toward his office.

The office is a vast, all-glass round space with steel framing and multi-levels for different seating arrangements. Above us is a massive atrium with a skylight and tropical foliage. The manager leads us to a round table in the center and we all sit down. I bring all the documents out of my bag, and the bank manager brings a tangerine out of his pocket. He starts to peel it as I introduce myself. He drops the peel on the glossy floor, over his shoes. Hongxi relays my story: a bank client, a death, an inheritance, no will, but two passwords to two accounts, one in renminbi, the other in dollars. The bank manager sucks on the tangerine, then spits the seed out of his mouth. It lands on his shoe.

你說你有密碼? he asks.

You say you have the passwords? Hongxi translates. I nod, looking at the manager's shoe, now stained with tangerine juice.

I believe so, I say.

你可以以提款機試用密碼. 如果通過, 錢就是你的.

He is saying you can try the passwords in the ATM machine. If they work, the money is yours.

The bank manager accompanies us to a bank teller. He explains the situation to him and gives him some instructions then bows to me and says, good luck, in English. I present all my documents to the bank teller and wait. He disappears into another room for a while then comes back with a big manila folder. He pulls the documents out and contrasts them with the documents

I had presented. He sits behind his computer, types, and waits for the data to download.

Mr. Nizar Faris Serhan? he asks me.

I nod. He types some more then disappears into another room. When he remerges, he has a stack of red booklets that look like mini passports, except The Bank of China is embossed in gold on all their covers.

他在全中國不同的分行有十一個帳戶.

Hongxi translates, he had eleven bank accounts in different branches across China.

Can I see?

The bank teller hands all the booklets to me. I open them and find multiple accounts, in Shenzhen, Guangdong, Wuhan, Macau, Yiwu. I flip through the pages. Seven-digit numbers, millions in transactions, unfurl before me. I trace deposits, transfers, totals, dates. There was a six-digit-transfer on the nineteenth of December, four days before his death. There was a seven-digit transfer on the twenty-sixth of December, two days after his death. Two bank booklets amount to $16,000, and the nine bank booklets amount to the sum total of zero balance.

This can't be right, I tell him. Tell him Baba was in hospital on the nineteenth of December. He could not have made any transactions at that time. Tell him he died on the twenty-fourth of December.

Hongxi translates, he is saying someone else must have access to these accounts.

Who? I ask.

The two men discuss this at length. The bank teller shakes his head.

> He doesn't know, Miss Mai. There is no record. He is saying, since you have the passwords, just try them now.

The bank teller accompanies me to the ATM machine. I walk and hear Baba's voice, he's whispering in my ear. He's saying something I once un-heard, and it's all I hear now.

> *Listen, Mai. I want you to know that if anything happens to me, you and your sister are financially secure for the rest of your lives.*

Reluctantly, I punch my birthday digits. I select English, I select savings, I select balance enquiry, and wait. Only $8,000 in this account. I enter Nermin's birthday digits. The bank teller was right. $16,000 is all there is.

There's a lot to do of course. Call the police, hire a lawyer, call the Lebanese Embassy in Beijing, the Interpol. I can tie all those traders and agents and business associates and righthand men and women and lovers and escorts to their chairs and unhinge myself, because I know how to unhinge, my father taught me. But I can't, really. I am spent and small, and this whole China business was never my size. I have no business being here.

So instead, I call +2 02, I call Cairo, my mother.

I can't, Ma. I can't.

May God forgive you, Nizar, she says.

She says it like it was no one's fault but his, like he'd committed some sort of abomination against his children, and I no longer have the energy to explain the maybes, the what ifs, and the whodunnits.

You've endured enough, she tells me, book your ticket back.

Shanghai, 2003

Return is a strange word. It presumes that people can be restored to an original place, to a homecoming. But there's no restoration here, only a brief respite where I can take stock of how I'm changed for good.

I leave Malik in Yiwu. Before I leave, I slip a few extra hundred dollars in an envelope and give it to Hongxi as a thank you gift, but he insists on not taking any more than what he's owed for his work. Before I leave, I bow my head to him the way he's always bowed his head to me.

I stop over in Shanghai, because a return to Dubai would amount to nothing but a spectacular crash, and I need to sit with the cracks first. To suspend my disbelief, if only for an interval, to call a blow a blow, give it a name, give it synonyms: grief, loss, erasure. I want to reconcile with this country the size of a continent. It is not its fault. My father ventured far, farther than his feet allowed. You can't walk into deep waters then blame the ocean for sweeping you. You can't carry all this baggage and not expect to sink. He made his choices; I will make mine. I will not board another plane with all this extra baggage.

I stop over in Shanghai because I also deserve to reward myself. Shanghai is a cosmopolitan city, a vertical one, with towers that touch the sky and spread their lights over the famed Bund. It was once a colonial city, under the control of a compound of foreign countries: Great Britain, France, America, and Japan. It has flyovers and *shikumen* lane houses. It has signs in English and bistros that serve french fries and cappuccinos. Shanghai's East to West elements reconnect my coordinates. Its cathedrals, synagogues, and Buddhist temples re-acquaint me. I walk through cobblestone pedestrian streets with boutiques, antique shops, indie record stores, and defunct factories turned art galleries. Shanghai streets are wide enough for me to breathe, and yet their crown canopies embrace me. I take a stroll, take in the diversity of this city. The trees are strong here, the leaves steadfast on branches. They leave my feet with nothing to crush. An outdoor café in the French Concession invites me. I settle on a table for one and order a pastry. I think of him. On my napkin I write,

> *How far might you go*
> > *when return becomes a place of no return?*
> *How far might you go?*
>
> *When your name becomes a thing of air, weightless, restless.*
> > *When you seek home in all the fractures.*

Night falls soft here. I wipe the pastry flakes off my lap and get going. I have an early flight to catch in the morning.

Part 3

Cairo, 1994

Our bedroom on Orabi Street is a two-state solution. Nermin occupies the left side. Books line her shelves over an unmade bed. She loves Trotsky and Agatha Christie, revolution and murder mysteries. In her free-time, Nermin reads the encyclopedia Mama had gifted her from A to Z, alphabetically. She's an old soul, dreams to the croons of Abdel Halim Hafez and bops to Elvis Presley. There's a sticker on Nermin's desk drawer. It's colored in shades of the Palestinian flag with a sign of victory. On her desk is a tiny cup filled with soil. I ask her what it is, and she says, it's from Palestine, a friend brought it back for me from al-Kabri. I poke it with my index finger, and it touches something unknown in me. I occupy the right side of the bedroom. I have a diary with a lock and key where I keep my love stories, a tall CD rack with all the greatest hits, and my walls are covered in posters of teen celebrities.

I make it into The American University in Cairo. The first two years pass leaving me to walk through long arched corridors, indiscriminately. I declare many majors, Mass Communication, Psychology, Political Science, but none of it speaks to me. All the words are convoluted and the pages are bulky. I consider following friends into Business or Economics, though I do not see the world of finance as one that could save the world, or save me. So, I skip classes and borrow other students' notes, until my grades fail me. By the end of my sophomore year, a letter arrives. A warning to my parents. I am on probation, it reads, and if I do not improve my GPA and declare a major by next semester, I am out.

By chance, I take an elective, Introduction to World Literature, and Mr. Dillon assigns *Catcher in the Rye* by J.D. Salinger. I write an essay about the travails of Holden Caulfield. I write, Holden cannot see the road, yet keeps on running. Holden is cocky, his cockiness protects him from world cruelty. I submit it for grading, and the teacher asks to see me. I am scared. I think my time is up. I put one foot in front of the other and make my way to Mr. Dillon's office, slowly. I stand in front of him, toes pointing inwards. He asks me to sit down.

Do you write, Mai?

Write?

Yes.

I wrote this, I say, in my defense.

Did you enjoy it?

Yes, I say, suspiciously.

What year are you?

Junior year.

And what's your major?

I squirm, I'm afraid I, I don't know.
Mr. Dillon picks up my essay and flips through its pages. I fiddle with my thumbs while his smile broadens. He takes his glasses off and looks at me.

Is something wrong?

Wrong? My dear, this is brilliant.

I go back home, my head full with what Mr. Dillon had said to me.

Nermin, I say, I need your help.

I cross over to the left side, sit on her bed. I tell her how Mr. Dillon thinks I should study literature.

Do you love it? she asks.

Love? I don't understand.

As in, did you enjoy reading this book and writing about it. Did it make you happy?

Yes, I say, but—what does one do with a degree in literature, be a writer?

Could be.

But, what about Baba?

Nermin rolls her eyes, Baba is in China, Mai.

Palestine, pre-1948

Home was, home is, an epic verse, beyond the range of living memory. A grand narrative of exceptions, lost origins, anti-heroes, and exiled journeys. The word *epic* comes from the Greek *epos*, as in, word, poem, story. Your story is about a home where words once held a flame to a big family. Let us build one home, they said, for everyone. Let it be the village pulse, a heart, big and roomy.

Home is a poem, every building block alliterating al-Kabri: A poetic meter in Arabic is *bahr*, meaning, sea. In October, before the rain, the women filed the roof with pebbles from the sea. Every October like a refrain, they filed and refined. The men dressed the walls in limestone and the balconies in fine scenery. They arched doors to the skies. Down below, the ground floor was carved from the hillside, into the hillside. The zesty courtyard flung by wings offered every family unit privacy. Each family unit had two rooms adjoined to the kitchen. The kitchen is where the women preferred to be, clamoring pots, icing almonds, and boiling mint tea.

But Baba, every epic also involves obstacles and worlds disrupted by the otherworldly. All epics have heroes and heroines who defy the odds, who break free. Breaking free, Baba. You were never meant to suffer in silence, to remain trapped in obscurity.

Dubai, 2003

I land in Dubai and go straight to work the next day. My body clock is four hours ahead and my mind is worlds away. I pop my head into Ryan's office to say hello, but he's not in yet. I enter anyway. Ryan's office is filled with flowers and congratulations cards. There's a Cannes Lions on his desk.

Welcome back, a voice says behind me.
It's Samer. He tells me Ryan had a big night and he does not think he'll be in today.

Why, what's happening?
He won a Cannes Lions. They partied hard last night.
Oh, amazing. For what?

I sit in my cubicle and google Cannes Lions award winners, 2003. My heart drops. It is a campaign I had worked on, written the copy for, but Faruk has been given art director credit, and the copywriter credit has gone to Ryan.

Faruk says, Ryan hired me just because I am a "hot chick." He hired me to look at me. These men seem to think it's reason enough to dismiss me, touch me, steal my credit, my money, and shush me.

I'm fucking fed up.

I call the son of a Dubai sheikh whom I know from sunset cocktails, nights on end, and after-hours parties. I ask to see him. We meet on a Friday morning in a café and order iced coffees. I have not told anyone about what had happened with Merzhad, so as I do now, I feel its weight shrink me. I tell the son of a Dubai sheikh everything, how Merzhad conned me, how he threatened to put me behind bars, to deport me. How he terrorized me.

Leave it to me, he says.

Please don't drag my name into this.

Mai, we're friends. You've done nothing wrong, that thug cannot touch you.

Promise?

I promise. Your story is safe with me. He will get what he deserves.

A few days later, I get a call from him.

Rejoice. He's been arrested.

How? What happened?

It was fairly simple. Merzhad has a record. He deals drugs, and you know there's zero tolerance for drug use in this city.

Everyone keeps telling me, it's not over, and how can I give up and return without my father's "fortune." No one ever calls it money. It's Nermin's and mine, they say, by law. Surely, it is not what my father had intended. Someone stole that "fortune," they say, there must be a ruse, a conspiracy.

Hiding in my office cubicle, I call an old school friend in Cairo whose father is the Egyptian ambassador to Thailand. I recount to him what happened, that Baba never carried credit cards, only cash, that he was on his way to Beirut to check into hospital, that he must've had a big sum on him to cover all his medical costs, that it all was mysteriously lost in a hotel room in Bangkok. My old friend promises to speak to his father.

A few days later, he calls me.

Mai, Bangkok is complicated, he says, its mafias and crime rings are entrenched within the system. They're tied to the government and the police. I'm afraid any cash your dad might've had on him has been stolen. I'm sorry, but it's going to be impossible to retrieve it.

Return is a strange word. It presumes you've been to the place to which you are returning. But return is a gene, dominant in the bloodline. It is what the children of Palestine do when they close their eyes, move past a somewhere, or stare at the trees. Everywhere I go, I go looking for my village in Acre, and when I don't find it, I close my eyes, I imagine it for us. Four springs, Ayn al-'Asal, Ayn al-Mafshuh, Ayn al-Fawar, Ayn Kabri, the largest water source in Palestine. Fertile connections where everyone is kin. I seek roots in images, in stories of return, and in this process of root-seeking, I become the maker of roots. I devise my recovery.

Israel, post-1948

Baba, I've been thinking of our springs, Ayn al-'Asal, Ayn al-Mafshuh, Ayn al-Fawar, Ayn Kabri: How the water formed diamonds on your feet on sunny days and a lulling circle at night to send you to sleep.

Let me tell you a secret about our springs. I read a book recently called *The Hidden Messages in Water* by a Japanese pseudoscientist called Masaru Emoto. Emoto argues that our consciousness affects the shape of water on a molecular level, that water is the blueprint of our reality. How we feel, what we think, and the way we live around water bodies creates different crystal formations within each water molecule. Emoto examined water from all over the world under a microscope: springs by croaking cicadas, oceans near volcanic eruptions, and rivers carrying the chants of Buddhist monks. He claims to have found that water bodies exposed to love, peace, and gratitude produced crystal formations typical of the exquisite workmanship of a jeweled crown, while water exposed to hate, war, and fear produced fiendishly distorted forms.

Whether this is pseudoscience or not, the book got me thinking of 1949, how Israeli settlers set up house north of our village and redirected the water from our springs. They called the new settlement Kibbutz Kabri. I wonder about the water there, whether it is conscious of its displacement, and how this violence might affect it. I wonder if it remembers all that it's endured.

I've read that Kibbutz Kabri sustains itself today through banana plantations and avocado groves, and all that reminds me of is Palestinians and Palestinian soil. I think of those Palestinians who died on a May Day, who've decomposed in the soil along with the worms, twigs, and flower petals. I think of how their traces persist in the soil, and how that might affect the taste of the bananas, the avocados.

I've learnt that the beeswax once used to light up your roads in honey tones is now produced in a wax-casting factory. There's a plastic factory there too now, and a restaurant and an auditorium and a horse stable. I wonder about the genealogy of the horses, whether they remember something, anything. There is also a reserve, a popular hiking spot along roads flecked with castle ruins. Tripadvisor says: During the winter, rain fills the channel and springs along the reserve's riverbed. All I can think of when I read this is how they have it all wrong. During the winter, the rain doesn't fill the river beds, but the springs and the water tanks, where the cattle go to quench their thirst.

Limassol, 1989

Teta reminds me of Eastern European grandmothers, or the late Queen of England. Every Saturday, she leaves her apartment on Tzon Kennedy Street and heads to the farmer's market wearing a scarf on her head, "babushka" style. It's a large triangular piece of silk that she ties in a knot under her chin.

Teta's mannerisms change once she puts on the scarf to head out. She develops strange ticks. Something about her breaks. She shrinks and her back bends. The matriarch recoils around a sudden, inward fear.

But then again, maybe it is not the scarf. Maybe it is the fact that she is leaving her place, getting into a car with someone else at the wheel, steering the course. Perhaps it's about the road and the fear that it might be one-way, out.

There are other signs of fear, like when she sits next to me in the back seat of the car, how she mumbles versus from the Quran and slips the tips of her fingers under my thigh. I always try to move my leg away, but her fingers follow me. Eventually, I relent, uncomfortably, and the warmth of my body, anchoring her hand down, reassuring her of my presence, carries her safely through the journey.

Dubai, 2003

I email Ryan saying I need to meet him, and would tomorrow morning work? In the morning, I pop my head into his office and find him there, dazed, un-fresh.

Congratulations, Ryan, on the Cannes Lions, I say, taking a seat.

Ah, thank you, he says, thank you very much, darling.

Wish I was here to celebrate with you.

Oh, you were missed.

. . . or for you actually to celebrate with me.

There'll be plenty more to come, he says sweetly.

. . . only because I wrote the copy for that campaign that won.

Ryan sits up straight. He laughs, or coughs, or something in between.

You—

Yes, I did.

You're only, you—

I slide my letter of resignation on his desk.

Ryan, Ryan, please. We both know it.

Mama keeps calling and messaging. She calls to ask how I am, what I'm doing, then messages to say she loves me. Sometimes, I answer, sometimes I don't. One time, I find a message from her, a holy quote, a hadith-Qudsi. It reads as follows:

> *Son of Adam, you've been created to worship, so beware of diversions. I've preordained, so do not drain yourself. If you accept your lot, you shall put your mind and body at ease, you shall be a grateful one to Me. If you do not accept, by My power and glory, you will never stop running in the wild, chasing like a wild beast.*

Cairo, 2003

I quit Dubai and return to Cairo, where my story is now fodder for gossip. At a party, my friend's drunken father comes faltering toward me. He tells me how my decision to quit searching for my father's "fortune" is a grave mistake.

I mean how many millions, he says, his body swaying, or should I say, billions?

I think of a billion bucks and what I would've done with a billion bucks. I'd be a nomad on steroids, no doubt, straying on high-speed, trading all the legwork for stretchy cars or a yacht, sitting in the back seat of a Maybach or sipping an electric blue juice on a breezy deck, never finishing a feeling or passing up a diversion, chasing ghosts by day and at night lying anxious on a revolving bed.

I come to a conclusion—If I had a billion bucks, I would spend it all, and still be spent.

I do not live in the English countryside, the Paris Latin Quarter, or Imperial Russia. My name is not Elizabeth Bennet or Madame Bovary or Anna Karenina. Who am I kidding? If it so happens that I ever meet Holden Caulfield on the street, he would not recognize me.

Who are you?

Mai.

Mai what?

Serhan.

Sarhan? he would ask.

Serhan, I would tell him.

Huh?

Never mind, it's a small difference.

Cairo, 2003

I get a call from Malik.

    I am sorry for your loss, he says.

    Baba's death anniversary passed, I want to say, what's he on about now. Instead, I garble a *thank you*.

    She lived longer than Nizar and still never learned about his death. He never saw her die in his lifetime either. See Allah's mercy?

    She, who?

    Your grandmother.

    Teta?

    Oh, I'm so sorry. You didn't know?

Beirut, 2001

Baba, I was not a child pestering you about a toy in a toy shop. I hope, posthumously, you realize I never was. We outgrow toys, they do not survive, but stories do, and none more than this one I'm about to tell you.

Back in Cairo, I began a master's degree in Arabic literature. I signed up for a class on alternative histories of occupation in the modern Arabic novel. I was assigned Elias Khoury's *Gate of the Sun*. It was an intimidating novel to start, 544 pages, but it was about Palestine and Palestinians, and I was told it was "epic." Reviews described it as the most comprehensive fictional treatment of the Palestinian Nakbah of 1948.

The story goes as such: Palestine is lost. Now, in a makeshift hospital on the outskirts of Beirut, Younes, an ageing Palestinian freedom fighter, lies in a coma. His spiritual son, Dr. Khaleel, nurses the older man by weaving the stories of Palestinians from town to town. Every night, Younes is kept alive by a story.

To tell the story, then, is to resist death.

I laid in bed reading, getting to know old neighbors, flipping through towns, passing through battles and falling into love stories. On page 166, I found myself sitting up straight. There, on the page, our small village. I found al-Kabri. "If we fought throughout Palestine the way al-Kabri fought," it read, "we would not have lost the country."

Never before had I thought such validation was required. Palestine had always been a series of obscure and interrupted images: You lining us up in Beirut and asking us to step forward, say our full names and where we're from. You mad at me for not knowing the difference between yogurt and milk in your, or my, dialect; a slap on the face in China for speaking words you misunderstood, a wine cellar, horse stables.

But there, right there, a connection was materializing in a way I never thought vital to my existence. I continued to read, to leave the edges and be drawn into the center, to the origin story, my story. On page 168, I found this passage: "At the beginning of February, a band of Israelis attacked the village and tried to blow up the house of Faris Serhan." Then again, on page 172, one old Palestinian villager relates a story about his forced displacement from the village. How when they ran out on foot toward the border, the Haganah stopped them in their tracks and showed them a picture of Faris Serhan: "He showed me a picture of Faris Serhan, and asked if I knew him. 'Tell Faris we'll occupy all of Palestine and catch up with him in Lebanon.'"

I put the book down and a scream escaped me. Mama came rushing into my bedroom. She thought something terribly bad had happened. I held the book up, but I had lost the page.

What is it?

Jeddo, Mama, Jeddo.

What?

Baba, your father, my grandfather, was the leader of the entire north of Palestine. You never told me. He built this village, developed it, fought for its kind and brave people. He gave it everything it had given him back. I found it all in a story, never from you. You couldn't tell me any of it and it no longer matters. It doesn't matter, because by some strange design, here I am telling the story.

Me, a mongrel by coercion, by war, with a border cutting through me, a fault line in the world's morality, a rupture, a runt, with a Palestinian gut.

Hong Kong, 2002

It's February and Liu Jianlun, a sixty-four-year-old medical doctor, is traveling to Hong Kong to attend a family wedding. Other wedding guests arrive from Singapore, Toronto, and Hanoi. Jianlun and his family check into room 911 of the Metropole Hotel. Over the next 24 hours, Jianlun develops symptoms, a fever, a headache, difficulty breathing. Despite feeling weak, Jianlun decides to attend the wedding.

The next morning, Liu's condition worsens. He can no longer breathe and needs to be put on a ventilator. Alarmed, his family rushes him to a hospital in Hong Kong as all the other guests board planes to different destinations. At the hospital, Liu's wife falls ill too. The twelve guests landing in different cities also develop symptoms. Two weeks later, Jianlun and his wife die of respiratory failure.

Cairo, 2003

My cousin Zena is in Amman when she starts a chat with me on Instant Messenger. She starts violence. She asks me how I'm holding up after Baba, and then asks me about his money.

    I told you, I never found money, I type.

    No one believes you, she writes.

    What do you mean?

    I mean, everyone in our family is talking about how you found the money and that you're lying.

I respond by blocking Zena.

Malik calls to check on me. He tells me his business is not picking up, and goddamn Beirut and its corrupt leaders. I ask him about Ou, and whether he's heard anything from her since we last saw her.

    Ou? Ha! Ou is a tycoon now. She owns a factory for children's clothing. She owns offices and warehouses all over China.

Israel, post-1948

Other kibbutzes followed in al-Kabri, Baba. Kibbutz Ga'aton was established in 1948 by Hungarian immigrants. It stands today on land belonging to Jideen that was acquired by the zionists as part of a trade-off with the renowned Sursok family in Lebanon. Today, the kibbutz boasts a contemporary dance company and a wine distillery.

There is also Kibbutz Me'ona, which was established in 1949 for North African and Romanian immigrants. I read somewhere on the internet that the one restaurant there is called Forest and invites diners to dine out in nature. I want to tell them they got it all wrong. There are no forests in al-Kabri, only endless orchards.

China, 2002

In December, a snake-seller dies at Shunde's First People's Hospital in Guangdong of severe pneumonia. His wife and several members of the hospital staff contract it, too.

Cairo, 2003

Facebook tells me to fill the parts about myself that identify me. I add my name, my education, my birthday, my work, my relationship status, the cities I have visited. For "Hometown," I try to add Acre, Palestine, but all I get is Akko, Israel. I try Palestine alone, and there are many:

Palestine, Texas

Palestine, Arkansas

Palestine, Ohio

Palestine, Connecticut

Palestine, Illinois

Palestine, Alabama

The only options in actual Palestine are Ramallah and Gaza. I go for Gaza, knowing full well the implications.

Palestine, 1948

They drill it into you.
You left, you left, you left.

But your leaders never issued an evacuation order. There simply is no evidence of one. In fact, there is plenty of evidence that the men were ordered to stay. On March 8, 1948, Faris Serhan, along with members of the Arab Higher Committee, circulated a memorandum to all the heads of Arab governments urging them not to grant entry permits into Arab countries to any Palestinians with the exception of students, people traveling for health reasons, and delegates of the committee itself. The memorandum also requested the heads of Arab governments not to renew the residency permits of Palestinians already living in Arab countries. On April 11, 1948, just after the massacre of Deir Yassin, a scribble was written in haste on the back of a leave permit issued by the Arab Commander of the Jerusalem district. It urged the headmen of the village of Suba to remain calm and have no fear for their women and children. On April 22, 1948, the Palestinian newspaper al-Difa' published a statement by the Arab Higher Committee which, far from asking men to leave, asked them to be patient and to hold their ground. It read: The duty of the defense of the Holy Land rests upon us, the people of Palestine, first and foremost. On May 15, 1948, the Arab radio issued three statements. The first urged members of the Supreme Muslim Council, the officials of the Muslim courts, and the sheikhs to continue their duties. The second asked officials of the prison department to continue their duties. The third requested that all Arab officials remain at their posts.[3]

You did not leave, Baba, your mother was terrorized into leaving. She ran because the Haganah left dynamite in her house. She ran because the whole village ran, ran for its life, past springs that exploded into a million droplets. You ran crying, not knowing whether it was water, or glass, or both.

China, 2002

Huang Xinchu is a 36-year-old chef who works at a local restaurant in Shenzhen. He calls his family from work one day and tells them he's been running a high fever for a week. He tells them it's probably due to the nature of his work, being stuck in a warm and suffocating kitchen all day, and they convince him to come home. At home, Huang's condition deteriorates, and his family transfer him to Heyuan Hospital. Two days later his condition deteriorates even further. He cannot breathe. The family transfer him to Guangzhou Military General Hospital where he faints upon arrival. By the time he is discharged, eight doctors are infected by a mysterious respiratory disease.

Cairo, 2003

I tell a friend about a recurrent dream that just won't let me be. I dream of my father, frail, moving across a small room. He is half world, half the color morgue. He is cold and all the blankets in the world won't warm his bones. I know he won't rest until he tells me something, but he just cannot speak.

My friend gifts me a session with a clairvoyant. I meet her and ask, what is it that Baba is trying to tell me? She summons him to the room and I sit still, watch her face contort, wait for her to open her eyes. With her eyes closed, she tells me my father comes with others, bad spirits that aren't welcome, they won't let him speak. She tells me if they do not leave, she will have to end our session. She mutters words in code.

Who are they? I ask.

Some gang, she says, a crime ring? Wait.

A few minutes pass and her face is released from its creases. She tells me he's alone with us now. She tells me the circumstances of his death were dark and dangerous and complicated. There were people involved, people who took everything, who could harm me.

It is in your hands, Mai.

What is?

That room he's in, the half world, she says, now
opening her eyes.

Is he cold?

To the bones.

Can he speak?

He's telling you to put this whole thing with the
money behind you. He will not rest until you lay
it all to rest.

I leave the clairvoyant and take a walk under a full moon.
When I get home, I light a candle by my window and
burn some sage. I get a pen and paper, but before I sit
to write him a letter, to release him, the letter writes me.
Its words are a warn flame that won't ravage me.

Nermin calls a few men Father: her old university professor, the editor-in-chief of the newspaper where she works. The father figures are a certain prototype, they're academics or activists, men who know how to guide, deftly, who know how to communicate, gently. In her home, she has their pictures framed among our family photos. I do not know Nermin's other fathers.

I meet her for coffee one day, I tell her it's time to forgive him. I tap into a lacuna, hear it rattle in pain. Nermin has no words for me, only tears, and her tears sting me.

> His anger was not about you, I tell her, it was not because of you, and it shouldn't have been directed at you.

But it's too late. Nermin, she's seen what she's seen, and she can't unsee it.

China, 2003

Chinese health personnel are alerted about "a strange disease" as early as mid-December, 2002, with cases in Foshan, Heyuan, and Zhongshan. A physician in charge of treating a patient in Heyuan reports to the local anti-epidemic station. In January, a report is sent to the provincial health bureau, which in turn distributes a bulletin to hospitals across the province. Very few health workers are alerted, though, since most are on vacation over the Chinese New Year. The same report is sent to the Ministry of Health in Beijing and marked "top secret."

The news blackout continues well into February, but word, like the virus, travels fast. People are dying in the thousands. Messages sent via mobile phones in Guangzhou talk of a "deadly virus," and words like "bird flu" and "anthrax" start to appear on local internet sites.

In March, The World Health Organization (WHO) issues a global alert for a severe form of pneumonia of unknown origin in persons from China, Vietnam, and Hong Kong.

Beirut, 2003

I fly to Beirut to spend time with my aunt, Amto Nadia. At her home in Tallet al-Khayyat, we eat manakeesh with sliced cucumbers and watch Palestine TV. There's a song playing and the sunlight is as bright as the lemons on the trees. Mediterranean scenes from Haifa, Yaffa, and Acre sweep across the screen. Amto Nadia can listen to these songs and gaze at these scenes on screen all day.

I interrupt her reveries.

I ask her about Beirut and what the early years were like for the family. Amto tells me about the first apartment in Sodeco by the Lebanese General Security building, crammed with the entire Serhan clan. The al-Qadis later joined from Tarshiha, and the families needed a space that would accommodate them all. They had to move together, and they did. They moved to a bigger apartment in Ras al-Nab'a and kept that sense of a ten-bedroom family home going for as long as they could.

Were they good times? I ask her.

Oh, yes.

Despite being away from home?

We were at least still together.

I had packed *Gate of the Sun* with me on the trip, so I bring it out and show it to her. I open it to the page with the yellow Post-It and the huge smiley face bearing the word "Jeddo." Amto puts on her reading glasses, then realizes there are too many words.

Read to me, she says.

I read about the battle for al-Kabri and how the whole village was stationed around and on the rooftop of Faris Serhan's house. "If we fought throughout Palestine the way al-Kabri fought," I read, *we would not have lost the country*." Amto turns down the volume on the TV and listens intently as I move to the next scene. Faris Serhan is in Beirut and Ibtihaj al-Qadi follows with her children in a truck. Back home in al-Kabri, the Haganah have a photo of Faris Serhan that they show every villager. I stop reading.

Did they ever catch up with Jeddo in Beirut?

They tried, she tells me, they tried to assassinate him once.

They were living in the apartment in Corniche al-Mazra'a by then, she tells me. She was studying for her baccalaureate. She had her textbooks spread out on the dining room table, the partition closed so she could focus. Suddenly, she heard a big boom, an explosion that shattered the glass in all directions.

Baba! she screamed.

Palestine, 1948

Hajjeh Fatimeh did not find the Serhan clan at their home, but she saw shrapnel chase the bobwhites, she saw their wings catch fire, and decided to keep running. She ran for four hours from al-Kabri to Tarshiha where she thought she might find Ibtihaj al-Qadi. When she didn't, she ran with the rest of the village toward al-Naqoura on the Lebanese border.

Hajjeh Fatimeh stayed in al-Naqoura for seven months. She slept under an olive tree from May until December, until they gave her a tent. Security was weak in those early days. There were no walls or cinder blocks, there was no barbed wire, and Hajjeh Fatimeh was able to sneak back into al-Kabri, into her home, from time to time. She went back to rummage for food in her pantry and bring water from the well that held the winter rain. When food ran short, water sustained her, until the supply of water suddenly stopped.

Hajjeh Fatimeh did what she could to survive. She walked for four hours to al-Kabri and found the well covered with a huge slab of concrete. So, she walked back for four hours to al-Naqoura empty-handed and gathered four men. She then walked back with the four men for four hours to al-Kabri once again to uncover the well.

China, 2003

Jian Yanyong is a prominent military surgeon born to a wealthy banking family. He turns the TV on one day and watches his colleague, Chinese Health Minister Zhang Wenkang, claim that the virus has affected only twelve people and claimed only three lives. Three days later, he picks up the morning papers and finds that Wen Jiabao, China's premier, has publicly stated that the government was fully capable of controlling the virus, before extending a warm welcome to tourists and business people.

Yanyong gets angry. Zhang in particular should not be making such irresponsible claims. He graduated with a medical degree and he must know the dangers of infectious diseases. Yanyong decides to risk his career, his family's safety and his status for the sake of telling the truth. He publicly accuses Zhang of abandoning the most basic standards of integrity as a doctor and proceeds to pen an 800-word letter to Chinese Central Television and Phoenix TV in Hong Kong. His letter goes unacknowledged by both TV channels, but Western news agencies catch wind. A journalist from *The Wall Street Journal* reaches out for a telephone interview, and before the end of the day, Susan Jakes, a journalist for *Time Magazine* in Beijing, secures a second interview.

Cairo, 2003

I sit next to my mum in the living room and watch TV. I flip between channels before I'm stopped by a familiar image on CNN: Chinese men and women crowding around food sellers in a wet market; woks and hotpots, feathers peeking from stacked cages. The news ticker reads: China Accused of SARS Cover-Up.

I turn up the volume. Apparently China has been hit by an epidemic. Apparently, it was hit as early as November of last year. The symptoms they describe seem eerily familiar: headache, chills, cough, fever, difficulty breathing, pneumonia. Apparently patients die within four to five days of developing symptoms.

I turn to look at my mother. I find her looking at me.

I am from Acre, but I write Gaza as my hometown on Facebook because of the nature of nomenclature. My village is not a kibbutz, my town is not Akko, my country is not Israel. I write Gaza as my hometown knowing full well the implications, the words, the rules. How the name Gaza compromises me. As a Gazan I am a Palestinian reduction, a philistine, an animal, hostile, filthy, a terrorist, a nobody. I reject the rules that form the names, because they do not fit. Those labels are all counterfeit and those outfits are made of bones, they're tight and outworn. They prick. No, I am not a terrorist, but I'm terrified of all of it. I am not Gazan and how lucky. I am free to go. My passport, cloaks, and me inside my invisibility. No 26-foot concrete wall to stop me, no ID checks, no checkpoints, I don't need your crumbs, your sympathy. All I need is a desk and a chair, and these words to write me. I'm not filthy, and I never was, actually. I have access to clean water, and I make sure I use it. The water I bathe in is for single-use only. How lucky. *Zzz* means sleep not an overhead drone, and *whoosh* is a skirt, not an F16 flying above me. I've never had to go on hunger strike to prove a point. I was never force-fed to stay alive, and you have yet to choke me. My troubles for the most part are existential not daily and I wonder why this makes me more of a somebody. How fucking lucky. I shall die once not every day, and I don't need to worry that God cannot see me.

SARS infected 8,098 people worldwide, according to the WHO, of those 774 died, and I bet you, Baba, you are none of them. In Guangzhou, you used to disappear into the landscape, you walked undetected down Wenming Road toward Da'nan Road, up Guangzhouqiyi Road and toward the streetfood sellers on Beijing Road. It's the route you took every day to see Lin. No one noticed you on the way, no one knew who you were, because all that you were could not be seen with the naked eye. You thought you were free as air, so the air played you. It carried in its stream something undetectable.

Something about that hospital let you know, you had to go. You had to leave all that behind you. Your arms there pinned to tubes that dripped, your yellow fingertips, your mouth muffled in an oxygen mask, and that half foot. Ou there by your side, something about her finally telling you, what's wrong with you, what have you done, and how could you. You had to go, you had to tear those tubes and bid fuck you to everyone trying to stop you.

On that plane heading to Bangkok, no one noticed you, no one knew what you carried, not even you. And before landing, every other passenger was infected, too.

You retreated to a hotel room, in transit, to a death, like you, suspended between borders. A single white room with windows like potholes. You did not die alone, you died mobbed by men or women you did not know. They snagged your pockets, they sucked the air out of you.

I never spoke numbers in your lifetime to speak them in your death, and I would never know what to do with a billion bucks, or so. You tried to leave me numbers, yet somehow I ended up with a story, which leads me to say, thank you. This story and its words, beyond what you left and how you left, these verbs are proof you were, once, and that you always will be.

Cairo, 2003

It's Christmas, the second death anniversary. I grab a chair and sit at a desk—then something dings. A notification for an email. I click on my inbox and I find, I find the name Nizar Serhan in bold black with no subject line.

I open it, foregoing all possibilities but one, that it is indeed, by some miracle, an email from Baba. I open it and find one word, all caps and oversized font:

HELLO

Who are you? I write back.

I wait for a reply—but it never comes.

Notes

1. Some names have been changed for privacy.
2. Kenneth W. Stein. "The Jewish National Fund: Land Purchase Methods and Priorities, 1924–1936." *Middle Eastern Studies* Vol. 20, no. 2 (1984): pp. 190–205. https://www.jstor.org/stable/4282996.
3. Khalidi, Walid. "Why Did the Palestinians Leave, Revisited." *Journal of Palestine Studies* Vol. 34, no 2 (2005): p. 42–54. https://doi.org/10.1525/jps.2005.34.2.042.

Acknowledgments

THANK YOU TO AUC PRESS, to Nadia Naqib, Nadine El-Hadi, Sue Ostfield, and my wonderful editor, Laura Gribbon, for giving this memoir a home and believing this very personal story of mine is one that speaks to many, and deserves to be shared with the world.

To Samia Mehrez, without whom so much of my formation as a writer would not be realized.

To Julie Wheelwright, who supervised and championed the writing of this memoir when it was still my graduation project from the University of Oxford's Creative Writing master's degree program; Peter Moore for calling his agent and saying, you've got to read this, subsequently landing me my first agent representation; the Red Cohort, Olivia Katrandjian, Iestyn Arwel, Georgie Carroll, Thembe Muvla, Alexandra Davies, Judith Norman, David Cummings, Ella Fidler, Ainhoa Santos Giocoechea, and Tina Juul Møller for workshopping the manuscript for a whole year with me and showing me its beams and blind spots; and especially to Sylee Gore and Nur Turkmani who care for my words as if they were their own and make me a better writer every day.

To the Narratively Memoir Prize, particularly Brendan Spiegal, and Alice Yu Deng for the brilliant illustrations which accompanied the winning excerpt,

I Have Never Been to the Place Where I'm From, But I Will Imagine it For Us.

To all the writers who have influenced my writing and showed me its endless possibilities; to Jeanette Winterson for the heat; Jay Bernard for the urgency; James Baldwin for the bone-clean sentence; Joan Didion for being Joan Didion; Ocean Vuong for vulnerability as power and Noah's Ark; Hisham Matar for *The Return*; Anthony Shadid for making me come undone on page 25 of *House of Stone*; Edward Said for being alive long after you're gone; Ghassan Kanafani for scaring them so much with your pen, they had to kill you; Elias Khoury for reorienting me to my family roots in al-Kabri, our little village in Acre, and showing me how ownership could be reclaimed through a story.

To my father's only confidante, Abu Fadi, who took me to his family home by Burj al-Brajneh refugee camp in South Beirut and gifted me a book written by Badr Eldin al-Jishi, a refugee from al-Kabri. I could not have imagined our village in so much detail without this gift; to Hajjeh Fatimeh, Abu Fadi's 94-year-old aunt, who still remembers, who told me about life in Palestine before '48, and what it was like living under Faris Serhan's roof; to my dear aunt, Amto Nadia Serhan, who no longer remembers much, but can never forget Palestine.

To Wael Omar, who was the first to tell me that this chapter of my life was worth turning into a story; Nermin Serhan for the courage and for giving me permission to divulge so much about our lives; my mother for the unconditional love; Sherif Ghoneim for stepping into the father role and treating me as your own; to my own children, my pride and joy, every day.

www.ingramcontent.com/pod-product-compliance
Lightning Source LLC
Jackson TN
JSHW022224240825
89837JS00004B/4